Improvise

Improvise

Unconventional Career Advice
from an Unlikely CEO

FRED COOK

Illustrated by Liz Fosslien

AN AGATE IMPRINT

CHICAGO

Library of Congress Cataloging-in-Publication Data

Cook, Fred
Improvise : unconventional advice from an unlikely CEO / Fred Cook.
pages cm
Includes index.
Summary: "Advice and lessons for entrepreneurs drawn from the unusual
career of a long-time leader in the public relations field"-- Provided by pub-
lisher.
ISBN-13: 978-1-932841-82-4 (pbk.)
ISBN-10: 1-932841-82-2 (pbk.)
ISBN-13: 978-1-57284-733-0 (ebook)
ISBN-10: 1-57284-733-6 (ebook)
1. Entrepreneurship. 2. Management. I. Title.
HB615.C6493 2014
650.1--dc23
2013048834

10 9 8 7 6 5 4 3 2

B2 Books is an imprint of Agate Publishing. Agate books are available in
bulk at discount prices. For more information visit agatepublishing.com.

*Dedicated to those who don't know exactly where
they're going,
but have the courage to figure it out along the way*

TABLE OF CONTENTS

INTRODUCTION

I am the CEO of GolinHarris, one of the world's largest and most successful public relations firms, with 50 offices around the globe. For more than 25 years, I've advised companies like Nintendo, McDonald's, Walmart, and Toyota. I've worked personally with Jeff Bezos, Herb Kelleher, Sheldon Adelson, and Steve Jobs. I've introduced the world to Pokémon, the Teenage Mutant Ninja Turtles, and the seedless watermelon. I've flown millions of miles to dozens of exotic countries, where I've slept in five-star hotels and dined in gourmet restaurants with dignitaries, scholars, and movie stars. Best of all, every day I get to work with a dynamic group of people whose average age is twentysomething.

Does this sound like something you'd like to do? Then answer these questions...

- Are your parents wealthy and well connected?
- Did you graduate in the top 10 percent of your class?
- Did you receive an MBA from an Ivy League college?
- Have you landed a dream job at the perfect company?

- Are you well on your way to achieving your concrete career goals?

If you answered no to every question, don't worry. I did, too. I never imagined I would become a CEO. I lacked all the necessary ingredients. I attended three mediocre colleges, received average grades, and acquired no legitimate skills. My experiences became my credentials.

Before I began my career in PR, I worked at a dozen enlightening jobs including pool hustler, Italian leather salesman, cabin boy, rock and roll record company executive, chauffeur for drunks, cross-country tour guide, junior high teacher, and doorman at a four-star hotel. Although I may not have realized it at the time, each one taught me a profound lesson that inspired my corporate career.

In the following pages, I share a handful of my exploits (those suitable for print) from which I try to distill some helpful insight. Don't think of it as advice. Advice implies the person giving it is an authority, which I'm not. Consider my musings as small signs along the road that point in a different direction. You can follow or ignore them.

Improvising with my life has given me a deep appreciation for people who are attempting to figure out where their paths lead, whether they're 20 years old or 50. If you're one of them, I hope this book will encourage you to take something ordinary and make it special.

take something
ORDINARY   &   make it
SPECIAL

1.
Expose Yourself

People entering the business world today are a commodity. They've gone to the same schools, taken the same courses, read the same books, and watched the same movies. Every summer they've dutifully worked at internships in their chosen field in hopes of landing the perfect job the day they graduate from college.

Meanwhile, companies like mine are desperately seeking fresh minds to help them navigate the massive cultural and technological changes they're facing. Where will they find distinctive individuals with diverse points of view to meet these challenges? China? India? Brazil? They shouldn't have to look that far.

While a college education is a prerequisite for most jobs, a life education should also be required. School delivers information. Life delivers ideas. Ideas that drive business. Twitter was an idea. Red Bull was an idea. *South Park* was an idea.

When I participate on industry panels, someone in the audience always asks what attributes make for a successful employee. My fellow panelists rightly answer that they're looking for skilled writers, articulate communicators, and aggressive self-starters. My response? I would trade ten of the above for one person with a big idea. But brilliant ideas aren't created in a vacuum. They're formed by the experiences we have and the people we meet.

My life education began when I was awakened from a nap in Mr. Moody's freshman French class. Although I never found school to be very stimulating, I did manage to stay awake through enough of it to get As and Bs. But French blemished my academic career with a D. My tongue still flops around like a goldfish out of water when I encounter a word beginning with *le*.

I blame my proclivity for French on my father. He served in the infantry in WWII, marching across France mostly in the rain and mud. He didn't talk much about his stint in the service, but I did glean a few bits of intelligence over the years. At one point, he was reported missing in action and presumed dead. Hearing this news, which was also reported in the local newspaper, his parents "buried" him even though there was no body. Later it turned out he wasn't really dead. After escaping a German blitz-krieg, he'd been living with a family in the south of France. This is where he began appreciating the French language.

The only evidence of this critical period in my father's young life is a German Luger he kept in his closet and an old scrap-book filled with black and white photographs whose serrated edges were held in place with little black corners glued to the pages. Most of these pictures are of him and his baby-faced army buddies pretending to be members of the Rat Pack, with tough expressions and slicked-back hair. The other pictures feature young French women in bikinis swimming at an outdoor grotto surrounded by rocks and trees. Like the men, the girls resembled young Hollywood stars, with long wavy hair and thin white bodies. These fading photos provided a peek into an exotic world of beautiful French mademoiselles and virile American soldiers enjoying the euphoria of having survived a war they were probably too young to understand. They also explain my dad's love of the French language.

Growing up in a small town in the southern part of Indiana, I led the middle-class life of Beaver Cleaver. I was the eldest of three kids raised by my housewife mom in a three-bedroom home built by my building contractor dad. She was the president of the Junior League and he was a member of the local Elks Lodge, where he hung out with his childhood pals. My grandparents lived across the street and my cousins at the end of the block. On my fourth birthday, my sister Carol was born. Shortly after my eighth, my brother Robert arrived. Our birthdays were predictably nine months after our parents' wedding anniversary. In the winter, we drove our Chevy station wagon to Florida for vacation, and in the summer I took tennis lessons at the local country club.

At the time, Bill Johnson was the best (and probably only) tennis pro in Evansville. In his college days, a newspaper article referred to him as a "chunky little sharpshooter" when he won the city championship. Chair dancing was Bill's other claim to fame. With little provocation, other than Elvis Presley and a few beers, he would leap upon a chair (or a table) and flail around in a riotous combination of the dirty dog and the pony. I frequently watched him gyrate a few feet above the ground at parties his students attended at his house, which may explain why he got fired from his teaching job after two years.

Bill took me and a few other budding tennis players on the junior circuit to tournaments in Decatur, Illinois and Middletown, Ohio. I usually lost in the first round, but my doubles partner, Tom Ryan, frequently reached the semifinals, where he beat some great players, including a 12-year-old Jimmy Connors. Despite my limited success on tour, at William Henry Harrison High School I was the only freshman who played varsity tennis.

That all changed when Bill interrupted my French class to inform me that I'd been kicked off the team. Even in my groggy state of mind this news came as a shock. He explained that the mother of one of the boys on a competing high school team had reported me to the governing body that cared about these things for participating in a "hat" tournament—when weekend tennis players pull names from a hat to choose teams for an informal competition. Apparently, I'd violated my amateur status by playing doubles with a handful of old men. My unsportsmanlike conduct disqualified me from every match I'd won during the entire season. Since I was undefeated in both singles and doubles, my team's standing fell from first place to last, and I was declared ineligible for a letter (the kind that goes on a sweater).

While *Sports Illustrated* didn't report my fall from tennis grace, it was a life-changing experience for a naïve 15-year-old whose identity revolved around hitting a fuzzy white ball, which led to a sudden U-turn on my road to the American dream. At this juncture my formal education ended and my informal education began. I replaced Harrison High School with Arc Lanes, a modern entertainment mecca featuring 40 state-of-the-art bowling lanes, a dozen pinball machines, and 15 pool tables. I don't remember the first time I set foot in Arc Lanes, but I know I went back every day for the next four years. I supplanted teachers like Bill Johnson and Marvin Moody with a new faculty made up of dropouts and derelicts with names like Red Dog, Baby Pod, and Fat Beckham, who were collectively known as the Arc Bums. The criteria for becoming a Bum included a high school diploma, no visible means of support, occasional access to a car, time in jail or reform school, and regular attendance at Arc Lanes. They affectionately dubbed me and their other apprentices "Arc Rats." The Rats were from a higher socioeconomic background than the Bums. We were still in high school and planned on going to college. Our parents supported us and drove us within a block or two (the respectable drop-off distance) of Arc Lanes.

I was the most obvious example of this cultural gap. As I entered my sophomore year in high school, my family moved into a house that my dad had built in Johnson Place, an exclusive 35-acre, fenced-in residential community he'd purchased from the widow of Mead Johnson, a wealthy local entrepreneur who'd made his fortune in baby formula. By any standards, our house was big. But compared to the humble homes of my Arc comrades, it was a mansion and a continual source of embarrassment for me. Many times, I tried to explain to my disbelieving lower-class friends that my family wasn't rich. We had a nice house because my dad built houses. If my dad sold cars, we'd have a nice car. It was that simple. I wasn't a bit different from them. But nobody believed me. Probably because it wasn't true. When I took a wrong step, I always knew I had a safety net to catch me.

The Bums introduced me to a new curriculum. English, math, and history transitioned into hustling, drinking, smoking, cruising, fighting, and sex. (I mostly audited this last class.) Earning the respect of my new teachers was hard work, but I learned a lot in the process.

Hustling. Even though we spent most of our waking hours in a bowling alley, no one cared about bowling. We spent most of our time huddled around the Brunswick pool tables arranged geometrically on ornate floral carpeting speckled with 50,000 cigarette burns. To prove my prowess, I wielded a 19-ounce, inlayed Willie Hoppe pool cue that my parents gave me as a bribe for completing the latecomers confirmation class at the First Presbyterian Church.

Mike Beckham, also known as "Fat Beckham," was the faculty pool expert. With his round belly hanging over the red felt, he could shoot a solid game of eight-ball or straight pool, but nine-ball was his real money game. Betting one dollar on the five ball and five on the nine, he filled his pockets with crumpled bills. I learned a lot about pool from Beckham, but I didn't play him for money unless I was feeling particularly flush or lucky. He didn't mind just playing for the time, which meant the loser paid the penny-per-minute charge for using the table. When we didn't have any money, we learned by watching others play for hours on end.

One Arc Rat could hold his own with any pool shark. Always sharp in his starched Gant shirts, Gary Gentry displayed a real intensity with a cue ball. Regardless of the stakes, he never played for fun, even with his best friend. I was pretty good back then and can still run a rack on a lucky day, but Gary conned me on the pool table and duped me at the poker table. I finally recognized when I was being hustled. Now it's not that easy.

Drinking. This was a required course and was normally taken in conjunction with puking. At Arc Lanes, drinking meant beer and mainly one kind of beer, Pabst Blue Ribbon, which came in many sizes and shapes—longnecks, quarts, cans, and stubbie glass bottles. I have no idea why the Bums drank PBR. Maybe it was cheap or maybe they liked the taste. But I know why we drank it. Because they bought it for us. John D. O'Connor was the guy who usually did that. John's nickname was the "Red Runner." Red because of his bright red hair. Runner because he made multiple daily runs to the local liquor store to buy beer for underage people like my friends and me for a fee of 50 cents per six-pack—a price we were happy to pay.

Whoever said alcohol is an acquired taste wasn't kidding. When I was 16, I thought beer was the nastiest liquid ever concocted. On many occasions, I remember wishing that this bitter beverage could taste more like Coca-Cola, but it never did. After dumping gallons of PBR into my stomach and regurgitating a similar amount from a car window, I finally got the hang of it. Too bad I didn't have the same perseverance with French.

John D. was my private tutor. Although he barely graduated from high school, he was the first intellectual I'd ever met. He was an expert on geodesic domes, photovoltaic energy, impressionist painters, organic farming, and Zen Buddhism. He was a poet, an artist, and a musician who applied his talents to being a bowling alley pin boy.

John wielded his superior wit to annihilate his friends. The more he liked you, the more he abused you. He nicknamed me "Dwarf," a reference to my physical size and mental capacity. No matter what I said, he responded with a biting, sarcastic comeback to put me in my place. While this may not sound like constructive communication, being hammered by John D. on a daily basis tempered me for subsequent combat with a lot of challenging clients that I'd meet later in life.

Smoking. For me, smoking was as difficult a subject as drinking, and even more critical to my image. In the era of James Dean, I looked like a chubby-cheeked Boy Scout in a Norman Rockwell painting.

Everyone at Arc Lanes smoked, but the honors went to John D., who invested all his profits from buying beer into purchasing cigarettes. He was a serious smoker who instead of puffing actually sucked on a cigarette until his red cheeks puckered. Unlike the rest of us, he carried one pack each of Winstons and Salems bulging out of his shirt pocket, his novel approach to blending regular and menthol. In either case, John D. knew how to inhale, a talent that took me a year to learn. I remember practicing smoking at a local haunt called the Surf Club, exhaling in all kinds of creative ways to make it look as if the smoke had actually made the trip through my lungs rather than just being held inside my mouth for a few seconds. Drinking came with puking. Smoking came with coughing. Acquiring these skills was not easy but I eventually mastered them both.

Music. This was a popular elective taught by Bob Ledbetter, who was the lead singer in a band called the Villains. Led could drink a case of longneck PBRs in one sitting and had the beer belly to prove it. But on stage he was our rock idol. The best parties and clubs (there weren't many of either) featured the Villains, with the rest of us as a drunken back-up chorus — wailing songs like "Louie, Louie" and "The House of the Rising Sun." The Beatles were preparing to conquer America, but the Villains ruled Southern Indiana. And I was eager to be part of their entourage.

Cruising. There was never anywhere to go in Evansville, which explains why we spent endless hours driving around looking for something to do. Harrison High School taught introductory driver's education. Arc Lanes taught the advanced class — driving while drunk. There was no special teacher for this course, but we all managed to get the required hours behind the wheel with a beer in hand.

Even though we had no destination, we didn't drive around aimlessly. We had a route. It began in the back parking lot of Arc Lanes and proceeded up Green River Road, past the Washington Square Mall and a growing stretch of strip centers, to the Farmer's Daughter, a restaurant where customers ordered burgers and fries from a speaker. And waitresses in short pink skirts delivered them on a tray that attached to the car window. This was all very convenient, but we never stopped to eat. We just drove in a circle around the people who did. After about 17 revolutions, looking for I'm not exactly sure what, we headed across town to another restaurant. More like a McDonald's with checkered flags instead of arches, Sandy's was a hangout for kids from a rival high school. After a few laps, we returned to the Farmer's Daughter. The round trip took just enough time to drink one PBR, which, repeated six or eight times, made for a typical Saturday evening. These endless, pointless journeys planted an entrepreneurial seed that would bloom in my future.

Sex. My sexual education began in North Carolina at Camp Sequoia, which billed itself as "A Camp with a Purpose." I don't recall anyone ever asking what the purpose was, but I deduced it must've been sex education. During each session, Chief, the white-haired gentleman who founded the camp, delivered a Fidel Castro-length speech to an assembly of clean-cut campers neatly dressed in khaki shorts and white T-shirts. At age 12, I didn't understand one word he said, but I'm pretty sure he was lecturing us about sex.

I assumed Chief had the noblest intentions, even when he asked me to appear naked in a movie. After choosing my cabin as the perfect setting for the camp's promotional video, he filmed my bunkmates making their beds, playing catch, and climbing a rope. Then he ordered me to take a shower. Since no one ever argued with Chief, I stripped down for a sudsy scrub exposing my awkward smile, red face, and little white butt. The only thing more humiliating than filming my nude scene was watching it the following year when the camp sales staff came to town to convince potential campers' parents they should send their kids to a camp with a purpose.

I watched with growing relief as the reel of film on top of the projector got smaller and smaller, and my cameo had not yet appeared among the scenes of wholesome young boys canoeing, singing, and chopping wood. As I was about to escape em-bare-ass-ment, my toothy grin and soapy rear filled the entire screen, right before the climactic image of the American flag blowing in the breeze. Brilliant editing for sure, but I wanted to melt into the shag carpeting.

Later, I took a more advanced course in sex at the Rockport County Fair, a pathetic annual event comprising mostly rigged carnival games that were impossible to win. Nonetheless, like pilgrims to Mecca, horny Hoosiers drove hours to witness the feature attraction—a live strip show. Crammed shoulder to shoulder in a small steamy circus tent, we stood in awe as the ugliest women we'd ever seen matter-of-factly removed their clothes, crouched on the eye-level stage, and began inserting random objects into their bodies. Having never seen a vagina before, I was surprised to learn they could eject ping-pong balls and smoke cigarettes. We watched in amazement as one woman borrowed Fat Beckham's glasses, then a few seconds later placed the shiny wet frames back on his nose.

The Bums talked about getting laid constantly, but few ever went on a date. There were a couple of girls hanging around Arc Lanes who were rumored to be willing to do it with anybody, with the possible exception of baby-faced guys like me. One was Fat Beckham's girlfriend, who initiated my fellow Rat Jim Celania in the backseat of his green Corvair. He immediately raced over to instruct me in the mysteries of intercourse, explaining that you didn't really move up and down like we'd always imagined, but forward and back! I stored this valuable piece of information away for later.

Fighting. When we weren't talking about sex, we were talking about fighting. But like sex, everyone talked about fighting more than they actually did it—except Dan Leinenbach. Compared to the rest of the Bums, Dan was the strong silent type. I'm not sure what made him so tough. He wasn't that big—maybe

6 feet, 170 pounds, with shaggy blonde hair and an affable grin. No one would pick him out of a crowd as a menace to society. It wasn't what Dan had that made him tough, it was what he didn't have: fear. He didn't really give a damn about much of anything, which made him very intimidating to anyone who thought teeth improved their appearance. Dan didn't teach me to fight, because having him around meant I didn't have to, which perfectly suited my personality and physique. I was never a tough guy, but I did learn how to act like one when I need to.

For every altercation I eluded, my childhood friend Michael McCummings jumped in with both fists. The Bums nicknamed him "Ralph" because of his large nose and puffy prizefighter features. Michael wasn't handsome but he had a certain rugged charm. Like Dan, Michael lacked the fear gene. But unlike Dan, who enjoyed his tough reputation without having to prove it, Michael attracted trouble like a puppy does fleas.

Michael was a constant source of amusement to the Bums because he would do anything. Jump off the bowling alley roof. Run across broken beer bottles. Climb into a manhole. It was liberating to have a friend who was so uninhibited. Together, we would do wilder things than I'd ever do alone. For years, it was all pretty harmless. But that didn't last.

One Saturday night, while my girlfriend Dorothy Parker and I were fogging up the car windows to *Viva Las Vegas* at the drive-in movie, Michael was acting out a scene from *West Side Story* in a school parking lot. For some undiscovered reason, the normally peaceful trip from Sandy's to the Farmer's Daughter turned into a drive-by argument, which escalated into hand-to-hand combat with broken beer bottles.

The details were sketchy but in the midst of a brawl between gangs from rival schools, someone fired a bullet that somehow made it through the melee of flailing arms and legs into Michael's head.

After I got word of what happened, I dropped off Dorothy and drove to the hospital to find Michael's mom sitting alone in the waiting room while the attending doctors performed emergency brain surgery. I wondered what the odds were that my oldest friend was going to die from a bullet wound. But he didn't. The surgeons removed the 22-caliber slug and Michael recovered. Medically, I have no idea what saved him, other than his thick skull. Now Ralph, the guy with a few loose screws, had a few new ones—securing a metal plate to the inside of his cranium.

During the ninth grade, I was on the tennis team and the student council. By the time I finished tenth grade, I was hanging out in pool halls, jails, and emergency rooms. My mother was worried and my dad was angry. This was not the life they'd envisioned for their eldest son. But I was hooked on a world filled with eccentric characters and extraordinary experiences. Early exposure to an alternative universe fused my future wiring. I was eager to install more memory.

Humans create original ideas by connecting existing information in new ways. The more data you store away the better. If you expose yourself to unfamiliar people, places, and things, you expand the personal Internet inside your head. Need a bright idea? Google yourself.

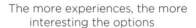

The more experiences, the more
interesting the options

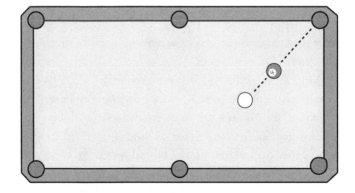

Think of your experiences as balls on a pool table. If there are only two, your shot options are limited. But when you have fifteen, the combinations are endless. Like many others, I work in a business of ideas, and I usually generate more than most people. I'm not smarter or more creative. I just have more balls. A broader perspective makes any game you play a lot more stimulating.

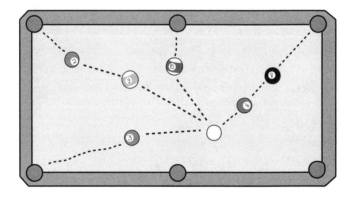

Stepping outside your comfort zone will also prepare you for customers and bosses who may not understand or appreciate you. Most of us like to hang out with people just like us, because we have a lot in common. This is a problem. If you spend all of your time with people who are like you, you won't learn how to deal with people who aren't (or don't) like you. If you've already assembled a cast of curious characters, learn from them. If you haven't, move to Las Vegas.

Sheldon Adelson is a different breed of CEO. Even though *Forbes* has ranked him number three on their richest-people list, just behind Bill Gates and Warren Buffet, he doesn't have the classy pedigree of his suave gaming-industry rival, Steve Wynn. Sheldon grew up in Boston, the son of a taxi driver. After dropping out of college, he sold toiletries. Then he started a charter tour business. In 1979, he developed COMDEX, which grew to become the world's largest IT convention. Sixteen years later,

Stepping out of your comfort zone
prepares you for the big bad world

Real World

Comfort Zone

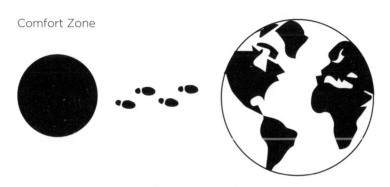

he sold the rights to the show for almost a billion dollars, which he used to construct his first hotel. He hired my company to promote the grand opening of the most controversial property ever built in Las Vegas—the 3,000-room Venetian Resort, inspired by his favorite city, complete with canals and gondolas.

Sheldon was feared by unions and disliked by power brokers. All of them predicted he'd fail, but that didn't bother Sheldon. He had a vision and was intimately involved in each detail of realizing it. He attended every meeting and voiced his opinion on every topic, often at the top of his lungs. When he was angry, he yelled at you. When he was disappointed, he fired you. But I was never intimidated, because Sheldon reminded me of my street-smart friends like John D. Instead of cowering at the conference table, I waited until he finished his tirade and calmly stated my opinion, which was the only way to gain his respect.

Despite his dictatorial methodology, on opening day Sheldon's palace wasn't ready. Outside, scaffolding adorned most of the gothic façade. Inside, workers were still decorating frescoed ceilings and laying ornate carpeting. The night before the Venetian's grand opening, the city refused to issue the hotel's occupancy permit. Undaunted, Sheldon commanded we carry on. It was time to improvise. We scrapped the plan we'd developed during the previous 12 months and transferred more than 400 international journalists to rival hotels. In addition to redirecting our team, my job included sorting out the media's luggage in the basement.

Ignoring the shouts of union protesters, we guided Sheldon and Sophia Loren past painters and carpenters on a tour of the expansive property. Along the way, he proudly pointed out every carving and crenellation. Finally, before a horde of camera crews, he helped his celebrity guest christen a floating gondola with a bottle of prosecco—never acknowledging that his masterpiece still needed a little touching up. He followed the Venetian with a second hotel in Las Vegas and seven more in Asia.

Sheldon is a demanding boss who does whatever he believes is right, despite what anyone else thinks. I don't agree with his politics, but my pals at Arc Lanes helped me understand that inside his rough exterior, Sheldon is a just a regular guy who knows what other regular guys want—whether they live in Vegas or Macau.

Being a little different will make
you stand out

Whether you're looking for your first job or your fifth, you'll benefit from exploring unusual ideas and engaging unconventional people. Being a little different will help you stand out. Being a little tougher will help you survive. Here are a few easy ways to get started.

Pick up a periodical

Think of your life as a big magazine rack, like the ones in the airport. When you are standing in front of it deciding what to choose, resist the normal impulse to reach for *People* or *Cosmopolitan*. Instead, grab a copy of *Game Informer*, *Inked*, *Guns and Ammo*, *Bass Fisherman*, or my favorite, *Scrapbooking and Beyond*. Each of these publications will open your eyes to other worlds where lots of other people live. People who may someday be your employees, constituents, or customers.

New options open new doors

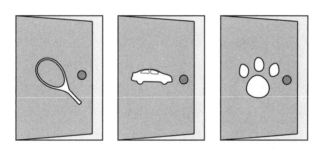

Take in a movie

Apply the same approach to movies. I thought *The Hunger Games* were engaging books and entertaining films with an original vision of the future. But so did everyone else. What could have been unique content became a commodity, replicated on T-shirts and elsewhere throughout our collective consciousness. Try seeing movies few audiences have seen—like *Waiting for Superman*, *Last Train Home*, or *Waste Land*—that tell real stories about real people in the US, China, and Brazil, who are also fighting for their lives in worlds most of us will never comprehend. Try the same thing on TV. Skip *Modern Family* and tune in to a Mongol family on the Discovery Channel.

Talk to a taxi driver

Cabbies know everything. Because they've immigrated from Russia, Africa, and Europe, they can provide personal perspectives on things like the conflict between Israel and Palestine, the financial crisis in Greece, or the civil war in Uganda that you will never get from a newspaper. Many were professionals in their previous lives, which gives them a different view of the American Dream. The next time you are in a taxi, ask the driver where he's from and how long he's lived in the United States. Get his take on foreign policy, human rights, or where to eat. A cab driver in Austin extended my ride by 15 minutes so he could explain the difference between Sunnis and Shiites, without the meter running. Even a short trip can take you to unexpected places.

Visit a museum

To many people, nothing sounds more boring than spending the afternoon in a museum. But museums can be eye opening if you open your eyes. Even Ferris Bueller spent part of his day off at Chicago's Art Institute. Any kind of museum will do—art, science, technology. The more esoteric the better. I once spent an afternoon in the four small rooms of the Maui Sugar Museum, where I learned how American missionaries and businessmen stole Hawaii from the natives.

Every new
adventure...

increases your
creativity!

Instead of racing through the Louvre on an audio tour, find one painting or statue and stand in front of it for an hour, until you absorb every brush stroke, texture, and emotion. Then leave without looking at another thing. I once stared at Picasso's *Guernica* in Madrid until I felt like I'd fought in the Spanish Civil War.

Listen to Limbaugh

Conventional wisdom advises against discussing politics and religion. But you can still listen. Political parties are among the most divisive forces in America. Their strident differences of opinion have crippled our economy, paralyzed our government, and affected every business, large and small.

Whether you're a Republican or a Democrat, you will benefit from hearing what the other side has to say even if you violently disagree, because someday you're going to have a boss, client, or customer who believes the exact opposite of what you do. Prepare by tuning into Rush or Rachel and trying to figure out how the other half thinks. If you understand both sides of a debate, you'll be way ahead of the rest of the country.

Find a farm

Eighty percent of Americans live in cities, while more than half of the rest of the world works the land for a living. Because most of us only see farms from the window of a car or an airplane, we have lost touch with our agrarian roots and values. When you live and work in New York, London, or Los Angeles, it is easy to convince yourself that everyone is obsessed with Bikram yoga, Magnolia cupcakes, and Christian Louboutin shoes.

Put on some Wellies!

Put on your Wellies and head to the country to learn how rural America lives: gun control means keeping rifles locked in a cabinet, treating animals ethically means caring for pigs and chickens, and climate change means crops will die.

Hertha Meyer, our director of consumer research in Chicago, spends every summer weekend picking and selling apples on her family farm in Indiana. She works in a major metropolitan area, but gains a unique perspective from living in a rural community that represents a different cross-section of America. By talking to her diverse customers, she learns what they worry about, who they trust, and what they strive for. Growing up in the country has also given her a deeper appreciation of the hard work involved in creating a high-quality product and marketing it in an authentic way.

My company represents the producers and growers of peanuts, strawberries, eggs, oranges, and avocados, who are fighting for their survival against immigration laws, pesticide bans, diseases, water costs, and government regulation. When you talk to them, you'll understand why they have little time for yoga.

Play cricket

The world's most popular sport is football, but not the kind we watch every Sunday afternoon on TV. The American version draws about 400 million viewers, mostly in the United States. By comparison, 3.5 billion fans in more than 200 countries follow Lionel Messi's every kick, which is why Qatar Airlines paid $200 million to stitch its name on FC Barcelona's jerseys.

More surprisingly, cricket is the second most popular sport, with 2.5 billion fans—five times more than baseball. If you're in India, the sports pages are filled with stories about batsmen and bowlers. In the U.S, it is hard to know the score.

Cricket has 5 times as many fans as baseball

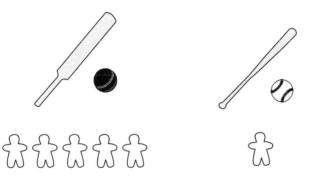

People around the globe are passionate about sports. If you want to know what gets them going, bowl a few overs, take a couple of wickets, or watch a cricket match on BBC. They only last for five days.

Go to church

But not your own. Religion is a powerful force in the geopolitical landscape, where a newspaper cartoon or a YouTube video can ignite riots on the other side of the world. And Catholics, Protestants, Muslims, Hindus, and Jews have been battling over their differences for hundreds of years.

Most people have little experience with religions outside of their own neighborhood. Their opinions and fears are based on stereotypes they see on TV. Go to a synagogue or visit a mosque. Read the Koran or the teachings of Buddha. By 2030, one fourth of the world's population will be Muslim, equaling Christianity. Understanding what others believe is the first step in communicating with them.

Ir a la tienda

Hispanics represent almost 17 percent of the US population and their purchasing power exceeds $1 trillion, which explains why tortillas are more popular than white bread and salsa outsells ketchup. We are all neighbors, coworkers, and customers, but we don't know each other very well.

Shopping is the easiest way to expose yourself to the cultures surrounding you. Try the neighborhood groceries in Chinatown or Little India. This is where you'll discover what people really care about—food! The typical Hispanic supermarket offers dozens of popular brands like Bimbo, Yemina, and Verde Valle that you may have never heard of, and sells fruits and vegetables like nopales and jicama that you've probably never tasted.

Have you tried these foods?

jicama

onigiri

plantains

naan

When Zandra Zuno, the leader of the agency's multicultural practice, travels to a new destination, the local supermarket is the first place she visits. She wanders through the aisles, like others might in a cathedral, to get a real flavor for a life different than hers.

Restaurants are also gastronomical gold mines. In most cities, you can sample Ethiopian on Friday, Korean on Saturday, and Vietnamese on Sunday. Your taste buds can travel around the world in a weekend.

Follow a leader

Most people use social media to keep tabs on their friends. They share pictures of their kids, their dogs, and their meals. Try adding some new people to your list. There are hundreds of business leaders on LinkedIn who are commenting on everything from CMOs to GMOs. Spending a few minutes every day hanging out with Richard Branson, Tony Hsieh, and Meg Whitman will expand your mind and build your career.

Occupy Wall Street

Wall Street may seem like an odd place to expose yourself, but reading the *Wall Street Journal* is the simplest way to learn about business. When I picked up my first copy, I was expecting to be bored by the daily fluctuations of stocks, bonds, and mutual funds. It contained all that data in the Money and Investing section (which I still usually skip) but its pages also offered lots of interesting, well-written stories about marketing, technology, politics, and global business. Since then they've added sports, travel, recipes, wine ratings, movie reviews, and a fashion magazine. I read it every day. So does every other executive. For its average reader—a 57-year-old male—the *WSJ* is the Bible of the business world. I've been in a thousand conversations that began with the phrase "I read in the *Journal* that..."

By scanning this paper every day, you can know everything that every CEO in the country knows, and you'll be miles ahead of your peers. Buy a copy or log on to the online version. You won't be bored.

Don't get weird

Businesses are searching for unique individuals with original ideas and global perspectives. But you may have to fit in with people who have none of the above. When you experiment with your life, try not to turn into Frankenstein. He was a fascinating character, but being interesting doesn't guarantee anyone will be interested in you.

Package your special talents in plain wrapping paper
(at least initially!)

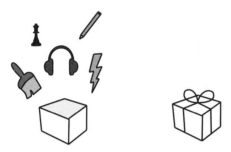

Package your special gifts in plain wrapping paper so they don't turn off the people you're presenting them to. Hiring managers rank cultural fit as the primary factor they consider when making new hires. In the beginning, you need to look and act like the people you're working with. Once you're established, you can reveal your inner weirdness. Imagine where I'd be if my bosses had known about my past.

As you mature, beware of habits—going to the same restaurants, watching the same TV shows, vacationing at the same hotel. Regardless of how much you enjoy it, repeating the same thing calcifies your creativity. If you want to stay relevant, expose yourself. Fresh experiences are the antidote for stale ideas. If you experiment with your life, you'll learn a lot about yourself and the rest of the human race. The knowledge you gain will keep you grounded and help you deal with those who aren't.

2.

Hit the Road

Americans are a sedentary lot. Only one out of three have a passport. When they travel, their favorite destination is Las Vegas. There they can photograph the Eiffel Tower, float in a gondola, and visit the pyramids. Less than 5 percent of US citizens travel overseas each year. As a result, they know less about the rest of the world than the rest of the world knows about them. This is a real problem when every cell phone is made in China and every

Percentage of population that owns a passport

US 36%

UK 75%

CAN 60%

service call is answered in India. If young professionals want to be relevant in an increasingly global marketplace, they have to pack their bags and get out of town.

I grew up in a small city in the Midwest—not on a farm, exactly, though I did have a pet pig. After finishing high school, I packed my matching Hartmann luggage that my parents gave me as a graduation present and headed south to the University of Miami.

Under the hot August sun, sweating through my dad's madras sport coat, I stared up at two 12-story, sand-colored towers, which were cleverly named 960 for the number of freshmen they would eventually hold. Turns out that my newly built dorm wasn't quite ready for occupancy. So I lugged my suitcases across campus to an "apartment" that looked like a WWII barrack, where I spent my first two lonely weeks on a cot in the living room of a concrete block building already inhabited by four upperclassmen. Waiting for construction to be completed, I passed the time at a theater across Dixie Highway, the main thoroughfare in Coral Gables, Florida, where I sat alone watching *Barbarella*, starring Jane Fonda, who at the time was considered by boys my age to be the sexiest woman alive. Normally, I stayed through intermission to rewatch the opening credits, when Barbarella removed her space suit piece by piece while floating weightlessly in her space ship, her body covered only by the little clumps of letters that told the audience who produced and directed the movie. As if anyone cared.

After no research and without ever visiting the campus, I had chosen the University of Miami as the institution where I would continue my stellar academic career. I figured it was as far away as I could get from Evansville without falling off the edge of the earth. It was also near the ocean, which must be why they taught oceanography.

I may have been the only kid from Indiana at a school that seemed to be populated mostly by people from New York and New Jersey. The alphabet introduced me to my first friends, who were standing next to me in a long line in front of our unfinished dorm. Not surprisingly, their last names were also Cook—tall, blonde twins from the Northeast. Between showings of *Barbarella*, I went with them to Key Biscayne beach.

My new all-Cook friendship was short-lived. One weekend I applied my Arc Lanes skills to renting a car, using the fake Indiana driver's license I'd fabricated on a Xerox machine at the library. I was gratified that such a crude document would permit someone who looked 16 to rent a green Mustang convertible and cruise around Miami Beach playing pool at the local bars. Finally I was having fun—until my new pals decided, since they'd paid half of the rental fee, that they'd leave me on campus and go for a joy ride. Feeling surprisingly responsible for a car that I'd rented illegally, I refused to give them the keys. Unmoved by my sudden sense of righteousness, the Cooks never spoke to me again.

My other "friend" was a snotty rich kid from Connecticut who became my new roommate in our eight-by-twelve cell. Despite being very close—literally, one foot away from each other—we had little in common. He wore a tweed blazer, smoked a pipe, and spent the weekends with a wealthy Italian woman who was a friend of his father's at her expansive Mediterranean villa, where she entertained visiting dignitaries and Miami socialites. I tagged along once and met the conductor of the Miami Philharmonic.

Our relationship shifted from tolerant to tense when I accidentally blew out his expensive stereo speakers while entertaining the entire campus by blasting the newest Moby Grape album from our twelfth-story window. Thereafter, every time he left the room he unscrewed his phonograph cartridge and locked it in his drawer. A few weeks later, I ended up getting kicked out of the dorm for throwing water balloons from my window. I didn't protest, since I was actually dumping the remains of a cooler of beer.

While everyone around me was soaking up the college experience, I was doing the same things I had learned at Arc Lanes—drinking beer, playing music, cruising bars, and imagining sex.

I missed my old buddies. They were more interesting than my new ones, and I was more interesting when I was with them. Desperate to fit in somewhere, I explored my final option — frat life.

In the middle of my freshman year, I once again donned my madras sport coat and made the rounds to all the fraternity houses during rush week. To attract and impress prospective pledges, the handsome, blonde, athletic SAEs parked five shiny new Corvettes in front of their house. Ignoring this warning, I signed up. My fraternity experience was fairly typical. For four months, the "brothers" tortured me like an Al-Qaeda captive, then suddenly proclaimed me their eternal friend.

I did actually make one real lifelong friend. His name was Gordon Woodward. Gordon was a local and not what you'd really call SAE material (a term used frequently in my fraternity), but times were lean and they needed the dues. Unlike the wealthy students from the Northeast, he'd grown up in a working-class Miami family. He mumbled his words, shuffled his feet, and slouched like he was searching for something he'd dropped on the ground. When we first met, he was living in a friend's garage that he'd decorated with Jimi Hendrix posters. I liked Gordon instantly because he would've fit in perfectly at Arc Lanes. And he taught me things I hadn't learned back there — like how to roll a joint, cram for exams using diet pills, and hold a record album without getting fingerprints on it.

Gordon and I moved into the fraternity together. With a can of high-gloss blue enamel and five sheets of fake-wood paneling, we transformed the worst room in the house into a veritable paradise. We lined the windows with two layers of aluminum foil to guarantee no sunlight would penetrate our reverie. To illuminate the darkness, we installed a six-foot black light, complemented by two Day-Glo posters: one of Hendrix, the other an orange spiral design that appeared to spin under just the right circumstances. We were pleased with our work.

Our fraternity brothers were less appreciative of our interior decorating, which was emblematic of a bigger issue. In the late

'60s, the pep-clubbing, Corvette-driving, beer-drinking values upon which fraternity life was based were under attack. Though maybe it was more a matter of apathy than an attack. Attack requires more energy than a handful of stoned students could muster. Gordon and I (and millions of others) discovered a new form of recreation that came with a whole new lifestyle as a bonus package. As a result, we lost interest in whatever had motivated us to join a fraternity in the first place. After a year of alienation, in the middle of the night I packed my possessions into my Chevy Impala and drove 25 hours to Bloomington, Indiana, where I continued my "higher" education at the state university. I was disillusioned that my first solo exploration hadn't ended well but returning home I felt like Marco Polo, loaded with uncommon information and exotic spices.

Back home again in Indiana, the Vietnam War—and my potential role in it—dominated my college life. The content of my studies paled in importance next to the daily death toll on the evening news. I was against the war, but I didn't participate in many antiwar demonstrations. Truthfully, I was mostly against *me* going to war. If the Vietnam War was going to go on forever, that was one thing. *Helping* it go on forever was another. I thought about being drafted every day. I wasn't afraid of getting killed, as that seems impossible when you're 20 years old. I was more afraid of contributing to such a giant waste of time, energy, money, and lives. The whole thing seemed meaningless. I didn't know a single person who wanted to go to Vietnam.

I did know one person who'd been drafted—Arc Bum John D. O'Connor. Unable to obtain a deferment for being the primary beer supplier to underage kids, Red Runner was obliged to serve in the army in Vietnam and almost died of boredom safely behind the lines. But I could never picture myself in a uniform, holding a gun, driving a tank, or playing in the Saigon marching band. I wasn't sure how I was going to avoid it. I was just sure I would. Going to Canada was popular, but I pictured hundreds of American draft dodgers sleeping in tents in the woods, which seemed a lot like going to Vietnam, only colder. Like my friends, I could've failed the physical by eating Dristan inhalers, or pretending to be crazy or gay. But I didn't think I would be convincing. To maintain my college deferment, I stayed in school. I chose to major in classes that started in the afternoon, because the only job I was worried about was the one I didn't want.

Dick Nixon finally saved me by inventing the National Draft Lottery, which changed the way American boys were inducted into the armed forces. He replaced a complex system of eligibility with a bingo game. On December 1, 1969, my friends and I gathered around the television set like every other draft-age kid in America (the ratings must have been through the roof) and watched as serious selective service officials reached into a large glass jar filled with 366 blue plastic capsules representing every possible birthday, including leap year.

The first capsule plucked from the jar contained a slip of paper inscribed with the date of September 14 — my roommate Rick Witt's birthday. A former Arc Rat, he was a funny, gentle boy who was already teetering on the rim of reality. Having his birth date engraved on the first capsule to be plucked on national television was a serious blow to Rick's mental health. After an initial blast of expletives, he remained quiet for the rest of the evening…and then for the next two weeks. Rick never made it to Vietnam. By the time he finished college and was ripe for the army, he'd been declared legally insane and ineligible for military service.

Having my birthday inscribed on the 250th capsule drawn from a basket was like winning a free trip to Europe — which is immediately where I went with my high school girlfriend, Dorothy. After a month of traveling from one youth hostel to another on a Honda 175 motorcycle and eating nothing but bread and cheese, we arrived in Florence, where a letter from my mom waiting at the local American Express office notified me that the local draft board wouldn't be requiring my services. This snippet of information changed everything. If I wasn't going to be drafted, I didn't need to return to college. If I didn't need to return to college, we didn't have to go home. If we didn't have to go home, we could stay in Florence. Since we only had about $200 dollars between us, this meant we needed to get jobs.

Getting a job in Europe can be challenging if you don't have a work permit and the only Italian phrase you can pronounce is *Quanto costa?* It turns out these were only obstacles if you wanted a *decent* job—therefore, not a problem for us. On our very first stroll through Florence, we met an American girl passing out discount coupons to the Italian version of TGI Friday's, catering to homesick American tourists who needed a Budweiser and a few peanuts.

Passing out coupons seemed like a terrific occupation, but she informed us that all of those positions were filled and suggested we inquire at a leather store down the street, located next to Florence's most famous square. Enzo's Pelleteria Palazzo Vecchio was the fanciest store we'd ever seen and we couldn't imagine why they'd hire a couple of scruffy looking non-Italian speakers to cater to their upscale Italian clientele. But Enzo, the owner and manager, offered both of us jobs on the spot. We were ecstatic. We could live in a beautiful city, work in the same upscale boutique, and get paid thousands of lire. (We later realized our pay amounted to approximately 50 cents an hour, which explained why we didn't need a work permit.)

Selling billfolds, I learned one reason why some Americans were afraid to travel. Foreign businessmen like my new boss were just waiting to rip them off. Enzo catered to a very specialized clientele—tourists. Despite his store's excellent location next to the popular Uffizi Gallery, we never had a single Italian customer. Ninety percent were Americans on package tours, who arrived in huge buses that barely squeezed through Florence's narrow streets. Like Michelangelo's *David*, Enzo's was a planned stop on a tour group's itinerary. But instead of admiring art, they bought expensive leather goods, "handmade in our own factory." Not to be outdone, we also had a "Michelangelo" (his real name was Chico) who used traditional craftsman tools to demonstrate how the 14-carat-gold Florentine designs were painstakingly applied to our purses and wallets, which were actually manufactured in the Philippines. At the end of the demonstration, the gullible audiences of gray-haired visitors from Iowa and Arkansas would gasp in amazement as Michelangelo rubbed off the excess gold leaf to reveal the intricate fleur-de-lis pattern on a scrap of fine leather.

The next 30 minutes would be like Black Friday at Walmart. Voracious consumers ripped handbags and gloves from the hands of the friendly Italian clerks to bring to the folks back home. Dorothy sold purses and I sold wallets—with a little fanfare of my own. My gregarious Italian colleagues, who could have sold gelato to Eskimos, taught me to demonstrate the softness of Italian leather by scraping my fingernail across the billfold and then miraculously rubbing the scrape marks away. It worked like a charm. After my sales pitch, our American customers often asked where I learned to speak such excellent English. To which I truthfully replied, "in school."

As our satiated customers reboarded their bus, their tour guide paid a quick visit to Enzo's cash drawer to receive a handful of little green and red bills—his cut of the action. This transaction was my introduction to international commerce, where in two-thirds of the world, bribery is an accepted business practice. Wherever you work, you need to know the rules.

Hitting the road will also help you understand why every company is banking on global sales to fuel its future. More than two-thirds of McDonald's sales are outside the United States. Boeing sells 80 percent of its commercial airplanes to international airlines. General Motors sells more cars in China than they do in America.

2/3 of McDonald's sales are abroad

But expanding into the rest of the world isn't easy. Every country has different laws and understanding them is crucial. In China, the absence of trademark rules allows local competitors to knock off identical products and sell them in the same aisle for half the price. In the United States, we're bombarded by TV ads for pharmaceutical products like Viagra and Lunesta, but consumer advertising for prescription drugs is illegal in every other country except New Zealand. In Sweden, mothers are allowed to take 480 days of maternity leave (which allowed one of our employees with five kids to avoid coming to the office for a decade) while Americans are the only workers who aren't legally guaranteed paid time off. In Saudi Arabia, for every foreigner you employ, you must hire a local, even if they never show up for work. In India, global retailers need more than 50 different permits to open a new store. If they want to sell thermometers, they need special clearance from the Department of Weights and Measures. All this explains why CEOs spend 30 percent of their time dealing with government regulations. In today's complicated global landscape, anyone who can help companies compete is worth their weight in rupees.

Less than 5% of the world's population is
responsible for 33% of its consumption

There was a time when Ford was General Motors' biggest competitor. Today, Toyota sells more cars in the US than either one. Whirlpool used to worry only about GE, until Sweden's Electrolux and Korea's LG started catching up. "Made in the USA" is no longer the gold standard, but Americans still buy more stuff than anyone else. Consumers in the US account for less than 5 percent of the world's population, but are responsible for 33 percent of its consumption. And 60 percent of what Americans buy comes from overseas, compared to 8 percent in 1960, when we bought a total of 300 Toyotas. Whether you work for Apple or Samsung, you need to understand your competition.

Growing up in the US, I assumed other governments operated like ours, until I lived in Greece when it was ruled by a military dictatorship. After two months of selling leather, Dorothy and I collected $600 for 60 consecutive days of work and headed south.

Crete, the largest and southernmost Greek island, is a rugged place sparsely populated with rugged people. Its Minoan culture was an impressive precursor to the Hellenic civilization that sprouted in Athens centuries later. But we didn't know that. As usual, we didn't know anything about our destination except that we assumed it was a warm place to spend the winter. As it turned out, we were wrong about that, too. Since Crete is about the same latitude as Nashville, Tennessee, it's not exactly a tropical destination. While cruising around the 160-mile-wide island, we stumbled upon a picturesque fishing village named Plakias, which consisted of a cluster of about 30 small, whitewashed stucco cottages grouped at the end of a pristine sand beach.

We discovered that most of the homes were boarded up for the winter, except for one that appeared to be abandoned. Through a wooden plank door, we entered an empty ten-by-fifteen room with a dirt floor and a small window. We decided to ask someone if we could move in.

A concrete block building near a handful of dry-docked boats turned out to be a primitive restaurant with three tiny rentable rooms on top, owned and operated by a small Greek man named Cristos and his large Greek wife, Kara, who were two of the village's six winter residents. After a brief conversation assisted by our Berlitz Greek phrase book, we determined that the abandoned house was owned by a resident of a village called Myrthios. Since our chosen real estate had been vacant for years, Kara saw no harm in our inhabiting it for a few weeks, but she did caution us about a leaky roof. Always undaunted by warnings, we rented two metal army cots from her unoccupied rooms and began refurbishing our new home, leaving our new neighbors wondering why "rich" Americans would want to live in a house deemed unsuitable for Greek peasants.

Our first step in home improvement was covering the questionable dirt roof with sheets of plastic that we purchased from a nearby nursery that grew hothouse tomatoes. We secured the plastic with big rocks that we found nearby. We also managed to scavenge a table and chair and a wooden trough that made a terrific sofa when turned upside down. Interior design completed, we climbed the hill to the region's only store and bought a kerosene lamp, a cooking pot, and a few delicacies like bread, jam, tea, and potatoes. Our house featured a small, waist-high fireplace for heat and cooking. This might have posed a problem for more sophisticated cooks, but since we only knew how to make Uncle Ben's minute rice and Campbell's cream of mushroom soup—neither of which were available there—the kitchen facilities were more than adequate.

I have a hard time recalling exactly what we did eat during my five months in Crete. Olives, which grew on every tree, were staples. We purchased a bottle of olive oil each week from our only other neighbors—Tasos, a 75-year-old man who looked like Yogi Bear, and his toothless, smiling wife, Boula. Yogi appreciated our business because once a week he got an extra 25 drachmas (about 75 cents) and a chance to grab Dorothy's breasts, an activity that turned out to be a national sport on Crete. We used the olive oil to make fried potatoes, which became a daily meal along with fried eggs provided by local chickens.

Once we splurged and bought one of the chickens, thinking we'd make fried chicken as a special treat. Because the chicken was alive, I had to chop off its head and pluck its feathers before cooking. Despite my gruesome efforts, we couldn't bite into the finished dish—not because we felt sympathy for the bird, but because it was just too tough to chew. I assumed we'd either bought an elderly bird or had omitted an important step in its preparation. I made a similar culinary faux pas when I attempted to make fried rice for two American girls visiting from Connecticut. This time I slowly sautéed the rice in a frying pan with olive oil just as I imagined a recipe would instruct, but the rice just turned crunchy and brown. Mary, the older of the two sisters, politely suggested that boiling the rice before frying it might make the dish more edible.

Over time, I did learn how to prepare a mean lentil soup, cooking the beans all day with a mixture of *horta* (a Greek word for herbs), which were really dandelion leaves that the local women picked by the apron full from the surrounding fields. For a night out on the town, we would join Cristos and Kara for dinner at their restaurant, which featured a familiar menu of fried potatoes and eggs, accompanied by a dessert of sweet, chewy baklava.

Despite our Spartan accommodations and limited culinary options, we lived a life of idyllic leisure in Plakias. Without a single responsibility and almost no human contact (or more accurately, conversation) we spent each day reading, hiking, meditating, and simply enjoying the passing of time. My only brush with work was repainting the names on the bows of all the local fishing boats. Thanks to two years of mechanical drawing classes, where I dreamed of being an architect only to be kicked out for being a smart-ass, I was very good at lettering. I provided this service for free, which enhanced our local status from weird Americans who lived in a dirt house to weird Americans who could draw a straight line.

A month into our stay on Crete, the rains came and we discovered why our house had been abandoned. Asleep late at night, we felt a few drops of water on our exposed heads. By the time we lit the kerosene lamp, the drops had turned to streams of mud pouring down from the ceiling. It only took a minute to realize that the villagers' warnings were real and our innovative plastic solution had failed. We grabbed our sleeping bags and slid down the muddy hill before the entire house collapsed. Covered with mud with nowhere else to go, we knocked on Kara's front door. She laughed knowingly as she invited us in for the night. The next day, after the rain had stopped, I climbed back up to rescue our dirt-covered possessions. Since life in our little house was over, we moved into the room above Kara's cottage for the rest of our stay in Crete.

The Greek government provided a bigger distraction from our peaceful island lifestyle. During the sixties and seventies, a military dictator named Papadopoulos ruled Greece. We knew his government was corrupt, but his totalitarian policies had little impact on innocent American tourists like us—until the day one of his minions arrived in Plakias.

When the military establishment decided our village of less than ten people needed supervision, we were graced with the constant presence of a zealous young policeman named Mikos, who every day did the same thing everyone else there did—nothing. He wore a blue uniform and a white hat to reinforce his importance, while it was obvious to everyone that he was dangling from the lowest rung of the state bureaucracy. Without being invited, he hung around the restaurant, by the beach, and in people's homes. Cristos, the village patriarch, who was friendly to a fault, didn't seem to mind. One night, though, after we had gone to bed upstairs, he and Mikos shared a bottle of retsina and began to argue. The next morning, we awoke to discover that our local keystone cop had arrested Cristos and shipped him off to jail for speaking out against the Greek government. No one knew what this harmless old man had said in the privacy of his own home after a few glasses of wine, but it didn't matter. He was gone and probably for a long time.

I was outraged by my first encounter with totalitarianism. My first impulse was to pounce on this mean-spirited moron of a policeman. But since he carried a gun, I decided to take my chances with the courts. Dorothy and I jumped on our motorcycle headed to Chania, where Cristos was being held.

Not knowing any better, I went straight to the office of the chief of police for the western region of Crete to explain that an injustice had been done and demand that it should be undone immediately. Surprisingly, he invited us into his office right away. I could only guess he was either interested in seeing justice served, or curious about what two Americans were doing in his police headquarters, or had heard about Dorothy's breasts.

In any case, he was very polite. He listened to what we had to say and nodded convincingly. He promised to look into the matter, but told us this was really Greek business, which we'd never truly comprehend—hence the saying, "It's all Greek to me." We left Chania convinced that we had introduced truth, justice, and the American way into Greece's corrupt government structure and that once the military dictatorship saw the light we had shined on the case, Cristos would be released.

Two weeks later, we returned with Kara and her daughter for the trial, if you can call it that. Armed guards ushered our handcuffed friend through a massive courtroom to face a panel of military judges seated high upon a wood-paneled dais. In this overpowering setting, Cristos, a tiny man to begin with, looked like a mouse facing a giant five-headed cat. The trial was short—there were no witnesses, no attorneys, and no testimony. The judge sitting in the center asked Cristos a few questions and then sentenced him to six months in jail.

We drove back to Plakias in depressed silence. We reminded ourselves that six months wasn't an eternity, but for a frail old man who drank too much, it might as well be. We also realized that in the face of a totalitarian regime, we were totally powerless, the same way millions of other people around the world were powerless. We never saw Cristos again, but his plight always reminds me that few countries enjoy the freedoms we take for granted.

Countries with free press

In fact, less than 15 percent of people in the world today live in countries with a free press—the lowest number in a decade. Some countries that claim to support freedom of speech don't guarantee it. I was recently visiting Mumbai when a powerful political figure named Bal Thackeray died of natural causes. His influential Shiv Sena party declared that all local businesses should be closed in his honor. A teenage girl who innocently questioned their decision in a Facebook post, and her friend who "liked" it, were both arrested the following day, while a group of Thackeray's vigilantes ransacked her family's offices.

The farther you go, the more you realize that people don't live like we do. Being part of the 1 percent in the US means you make more than $350,000 per year. Being part of the 1 percent globally means you make more than $34,000. Three-fourths of the global population doesn't use toilet paper. You may not always agree with people's beliefs, but you should learn to respect them.

On my first visit to Iraq, I arrived in the border city of Basra after a 24-hour bus ride across the desert. Tired and dirty, my German friend Heinz and I were desperate for a place to take a shower and sleep. We tried a dozen different hotels but no one offered us a room, even though we could see from the keys hanging on the wall they had vacancies. After two hours of wandering the streets, we finally found a place that would accept us. After we showered and reclined our weary bodies, a young

Only 1 in 4 people use toilet paper

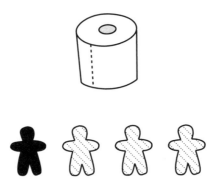

Muslim girl knocked on our door and handed us a small scrap of paper with a few words scribbled on it: "Sorry, the hotel is full, you will have to leave." That was my first experience with discrimination — an everyday occurrence for many people.

The world can be a tough place, but you need explore it. Here are a few directions to help you find your way.

Mind the gap

In the 1960s, the British created a concept called the Gap Year to describe the growing trend of taking a year off between secondary school and university. In 2012, more than 2.5 million British students took a break from school to recharge their academic batteries and see the world. The trend is also growing in former colonies like Canada, New Zealand, and Australia. But it hasn't really caught on in a big way in the US, where many parents cling to the myth that if their kids are sidetracked from school, they may lose momentum and never return.

If you spend your time off wisely, college admissions offices will find your experience an asset rather than a diversion. Plus, taking a hiatus can sharpen your focus and motivate you to excel. Studies have shown that "gappers" actually perform better when they return to school than those who stay. Recognizing this, 5 percent of US schools are now allowing for deferred admissions. Princeton University is creating a "bridge year" program that enables newly admitted freshmen to spend a year abroad doing public service work before they start classes.

Study abroad

If you can't take time off, consider studying abroad. In the 2012 school year, the number of American students studying overseas reached an all-time high of 283,332. That's a big number but it only represents 1 percent of the total number of students enrolled in higher education. By contrast, almost three times as many foreign students attended college in the US, which represents a 31 percent increase in a decade. 235,597 came from China, while less than 15,000 American students chose to study in that country. Most Americans prefer Europe as a destination and more than half only stay for eight weeks, usually in London, Italy, Spain, or France. A paltry 4 percent stay overseas for a whole school year.

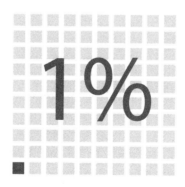

% of US students that study abroad

These numbers suggest that the rest of the world is global-izing faster than we are. Studying abroad is the easiest way to gain international experience and get a jumpstart in the global job market before your student loans kick in. Most schools offer overseas programs and many will help with funding. If you have the opportunity to study overseas, choose a destination that will impress your future employer and stay as long as you can. Spending the summer in Barcelona is fun, but Costa Brava is not the center of the world economy.

Get a Beijing job

If you missed the chance to study overseas, don't worry. Work-ing is even better, because the best way to understand the global economy is to be part of it. Almost every country, including the US, restricts foreign workers. You can follow their rules or ex-plore alternatives.

The easiest way to work abroad is to convince your employer to sponsor you, because the company can arrange your visa and cover your legal fees. When you are interviewing for a posi-tion, ask about the company's policy for transferring employ-ees overseas. Then explore your firm's international operations, look for opportunities to work with them, and visit their offices when you're on vacation. Once you've proven your value, start hinting to your supervisors that you are interested in relocating. Then remind them every few months. The process can be long, complicated, and expensive. But persistence will get you there. At my agency, we look for opportunities to move good people to other regions because it keeps them in the company and signals to newer employees that they can explore the world with us.

If landing a corporate position feels like a stretch, you can try teaching English as a foreign language. There are dozens of TEFL organizations online that provide certified training and even help you find a job. While teaching may seem irrelevant to a career in the business world, it will get you on the road and provide a paycheck. Becoming an au pair is another way to subsidize your explorations. You can sign up with an agency online and pick the places that interest you. Your sponsoring family will provide a work permit. If you don't need money, you can volunteer to work for an international nonprofit. The Peace Corps is the most well known, but other organizations offer similar opportunities. Some charge fees, but they can transport you from Kansas City to Kathmandu.

Find a guide

Or you can do what I did—figure it out when you get there. Despite international labor laws, if you look hard enough, you will find a small business that will hire you. Every major city has its own network of itinerant expats who can guide you to underground job opportunities. You just need to ask around. Since getting paid under the table may not be lucrative, it's prudent to have a small cash reserve to fall back on.

The less you structure your travels, the more you learn to improvise. I never planned an itinerary or carried a map. If I wanted to identify the local tourist attractions, I scanned postcard stands for pictures of Roman ruins or Hindu temples. I gathered the most valuable information from travelers who were headed in the opposite direction, who'd already been where I was going. They knew the cheapest hotels and friendliest restaurants. When I reached a new destination, I always found a guide, or one found me: not an expensive professional, but an unemployed local who made a few dollars a week escorting disoriented strangers around town. They were often street kids or old men, like Mr. Phillips, who took me through the back streets of Calcutta to see things that the normal tourist never does—including a burial *ghat* where a grief-stricken wife gazed silently through the smoke of the funeral pyre engulfing her dead husband's body.

Watching a cremation is entertaining but not really relevant to the business world, unless you're planning on becoming a funeral director. Prospective employers really don't care if you've seen the Mona Lisa, the Taj Mahal or the Great Wall. If you want your travels to lead to a better job, add some economic flavor to your itinerary. Tour EU headquarters in Brussels to learn how that organization keeps Europe afloat. Attend a seminar at the London School of Economics. Visit the American Chamber of Commerce in Hong Kong. Stop by Davos. Even if you only stay for a few hours, these places will make you look smarter than Leonardo DiVinci.

Learn a language

To be competitive on a global scale, you need to understand what the competition is talking about. After traveling my whole life, I'm embarrassed that I only speak one language, when many of the people I do business with in Europe and Asia speak four or five. English may be the international language of business, but that's just a lame excuse for being ethnocentric.

In high school, I only passed French with help from the unwitting girl sitting next to me. In college, thinking that language was an annoying requirement that I would never use, I majored in education so that I could avoid it. As a result, I have attended business functions in Berlin, Beijing, and Bombay where I had no idea what anyone was saying. Polite people will switch to English to keep me from feeling left out, but it's never the same as really being part of the conversation.

Learning languages connects
you to other cultures

If English is your second language, don't abandon your first. I've met many second-generation immigrants who thought English was more acceptable than their mother tongue and now regret they can't speak their parents' language. No matter where you're from, the ability to converse with your colleagues and customers is a big advantage in the international marketplace.

Even if you aren't fluent, a few words in a native tongue can pack a punch. Germans revere President John Kennedy because when he visited the Berlin Wall in 1963, he added four German words to his speech: *"Ich bin ein Berliner."* Fifty years later, that famous phrase is proudly displayed on billboards around the city.

Right now, there are 300 million Chinese people learning English. Not because it looks good on their resumes, because it's critical to their family's survival. Zhang Xiaoping, a 20-year-old English major in southern China, was quoted in the *New York Times* saying that someday she wants to work for a Chinese automaker, so she can provide the cultural insights and English fluency her company needs to supply the next generation of fuel-efficient taxi cabs, which New York City plans to deploy in 2021. "It is my dream," she said, "and I will devote myself wholeheartedly to it." Ms. Zhang doesn't look very intimidating in her jeans and ponytail, but I'd be scared to compete against her.

Bargain for everything

When you're a stranger in a strange land, people will try to rip you off. Get used to it. On a recent trip to India, a cute ten-year-old boy followed me and one of my colleagues around the shops near our hotel where we were buying souvenirs to take home. After a couple of hours, we offered him a handful of rupees for his assistance. We were surprised and impressed when he refused our money and instead asked us to buy some rice and milk for his family. He then led us to a street stall, where a woman sold us a huge can of condensed milk and a five-pound bag of rice for ten times the amount we had previously offered. As she put the food in a bag for the boy, we noticed that this was the only rice and milk she had in stock, and realized she sells the same rice and milk over and over to other unsuspecting tourists. In the end, we only spent $15, but we received a potent lesson in international commerce.

Local shopkeepers know Westerners have money and they're experts at extracting it. Enterprising entrepreneurs recognize foreigners will work for peanuts and that's what they offer. International consultants realize that American executives aren't familiar with local business practices and they take advantage of them.

In the United States, commerce is simple. Everything has a price and you're expected to pay it. Trading wasn't always so straightforward. Our forefathers bought Manhattan for a handful of beads. Today, shrewder Indians are outsourcing us to the cleaners. They're used to bargaining for everything. Not because they can't afford to pay full price. They just know they don't have to.

Start with small items that won't bankrupt you, like a Buddha in Bali or a bracelet in Dubai. Begin by asking what it costs. Never make the initial bid. When a price is stated, don't automatically think what it would cost at home. That is irrelevant. Make a ridiculous offer, perhaps 10 percent of what they asked. They may act offended, but if you stick around, they'll eventually make a counter offer. Then the fun begins.

If you have time to spend the next hour pounding on a calculator and haggling over ten bucks, you're likely to get what you want at only double its real value. Bigger deals take more time, and you have to be willing to walk away. I once spent three days dickering with an Afghan merchant over a sheepskin coat, leaving every day and returning the next to start where we left off. We finally agreed on a price and developed mutual respect in the process. A good salesman always makes friends with his customers because he wants them to return and haggle again.

Be prepared to negotiate professionally, without taking it personally. Haggling for trinkets taught me that you can argue your case without alienating your adversaries. If you simply agree to the other person's terms, they'll think you're a pushover. If you bargain, they'll treat you like a peer. In the end, the relationships you build are more important than the money you save. I've been involved in buying companies from people on four continents, and today I'm friends with all of them.

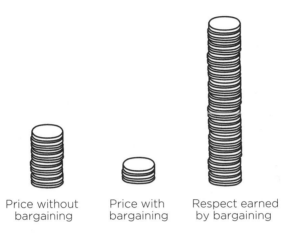

Price without   Price with   Respect earned
  bargaining   bargaining   by bargaining

Bargaining in an office is subtler than in a souk. If you're negotiating your salary, the parameters are already defined. When you're just starting out, you may have to accept a standard package, but after that it pays to negotiate. You can determine the "range" through online salary surveys or by talking to others in the industry. Once you know what's feasible, decide where you fit in based on your experience and potential. Pick a figure where you'd like to land and then ask for more. Always leave room to maneuver.

Raises feel more like birthday gifts. They come once a year and someone else picks them out. If you want to have a say in the process, make your case based on tangible value you've delivered. If it doesn't work, you'll still gain points for trying. As Mick Jagger reminds us, "You can't always get what you want, but if you improvise, you might find, you get what you need."

In my job, I am constantly bargaining with our executives, our clients, our offices, and our parent company. The process always follows the same pattern, which begins with a number, followed by a counter, and continues until we reach a compromise that makes everyone reasonably happy. Whether you are in a Turkish bazaar or a Brussels boardroom, bargaining is a requirement. Learn to love it.

Don't ignore parents or debts

Traveling the world is a valuable asset to any career. But there are a few obstacles that may prevent you from getting there: Mom, Dad, and student loans.

Sadly, American graduates owe about $1 trillion, an average of $25,000 per student. Repayment normally begins within six months of graduation and can last 30 years. That's why it makes sense to travel before or during college when you aren't grounded by debt. There is no magic trick to make student loans disappear, but you can work with your lender to restructure or delay your payments. It is possible to get a deferment by joining the Peace Corps, the military, or by teaching in low-income areas. There are also new pay-as-you-earn programs that reduce the monthly payments based on your income. A small percentage of borrowers move overseas to escape bill collectors—a bad idea if you ever plan to have a career in the United States.

Some parents apply more pressure than a collection agency. My own mom and dad were supportive of my wanderlust and would send an occasional money order to make sure I got enough to eat. Today, because college is such a major financial commitment, most parents are less tolerant, hoping their kids will secure a job before they even graduate.

In addition to money, your parents also have an emotional investment in your future. One of my clients confessed that she was embarrassed to tell her friends when her only daughter dropped out of a prestigious graduate school to become an au pair in Paris. When she returned after two years, her mother was impressed by her newfound self-reliance. Her daughter still wasn't sure what she wanted to do with the rest of her life, but she was confident she'd figure it out.

As a father, I understand the dreams and nightmares that parents have for their kids. I was ecstatic when my daughter Emily was accepted into Cornell and depressed when I drove her home a semester later. She never returned to college and is now happily working away at a casting career in Hollywood. I regret that her education didn't work out, but I sometimes wonder if I was really the one who wanted to go to Cornell and she was fulfilling my dream instead of her own. You may have to help your parents understand what is really important to you, especially if it isn't important to them.

If you can't get out of town, invest in a passport. Carry it with you to remind yourself that you are a citizen of the world. Put a map on the wall and mark all the places you'd like to visit someday. Explore them from the couch with travel guides, language programs, and the internet. Today, the world is literally at your fingertips.

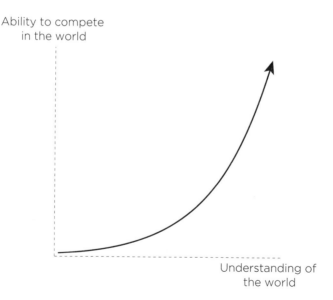

Since my first trip to Europe, I have flown 6 million miles and experienced many places average Americans may never visit again, like Burma, Afghanistan, Iran, Iraq, and Syria. On those trips, I've not only sold wallets to tourists and painted letters on boats, but also counted cars on country roads, peeled potatoes at summer camp, tested escape ramps on airplanes, and managed a global PR firm. As a result, I feel comfortable in most every culture and any situation. My time outside the US is directly responsible for my success in it. If you want to compete in the global economy, you have to hit the road.

3.
Ask the Captain

Every three months we recruit a new crop of interns in our Chicago office, usually a dozen sharp college graduates selected from a pool of 500 applicants. They're more interested in the hands-on agency experience than the $12 per hour we pay them. Their ultimate goal is to turn their internships into full-time jobs, which happens about half of the time. As part of their training program, they attend casual lunches to meet the people who are managing the company.

They always ask the same question: "How do I get the most out of my internship?"

I always give the same answer: "Make an impression."

Make an impression

I remind them that their time with us is short and they need to use it wisely. Not just sitting in their cubicles grinding away at boring reports but getting to know the senior people who can make a real difference in their careers. I encourage them to send emails, attend brainstorms, request assignments, seek advice—anything that will get them noticed by top management. Surprisingly, few of them ever do.

After these sessions, I might receive an email from one of the participants, thanking me for my time, but in a decade only one person has ever stopped by my office during a three-month stint, even though some of them sat just a few feet away. Recently, I received a handwritten note from a departing intern thanking me for the valuable experience. As I read the signature, I realized I had no idea who he was. I'm sure senior management must seem intimidating to those just starting their careers. But newcomers and old timers alike need to overcome their fears and ask a question.

★ Opportunities

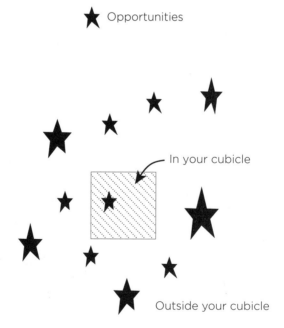

I learned this lesson in Hawaii. After a year and a half in Europe, returning to Indiana University and finishing my last year of college was the logical thing to do. Mom and Dad would have paid my rent and tuition, which was a whopping $350 per semester, but I wasn't interested.

I had gotten a taste of the real world and I wanted another bite. Unlike many of today's students, I had no loans to repay and no career to pursue. I figured IU would still be there when I returned from wherever I was going. After working for a few months helping my father build houses, I answered a classified ad placed by an elderly lady looking for someone to drive her and her three miniature poodles to California in a vintage Thunderbird. It was a perfect job for me and my childhood friend Michael McCummings. Three days and 50 doggie rest stops later, we arrived in Long Beach, where we slept on the floor of Michael's mother's one-bedroom apartment while she attempted to find us two free airline seats on the Hawaiian tours she booked for AARP.

Waiting for our plane to come in, we prepared for paradise by checking out Euell Gibbons's *Beachcomber's Handbook* from the local library. Gibbons, who had become famous for his living-off-the-land philosophy and commercials for Grape-Nuts cereal, painted an enticing picture of Hawaii—primitive grass shacks on pristine beaches with all the bananas and papayas you could scavenge. I'm not sure exactly when he wrote that book, but by the time we arrived, things had changed.

Our first stop was the island of Hawaii, where we learned you actually needed a reservation to camp on the beach. We also discovered that Primo Warriors—local thugs named after a Hawaiian beer—made a practice of clubbing *haoles* over the head while they were sleeping. Not to be deprived of our beachcomber's dream, we circled the island in search of the famous Wiapio Valley, which Mr. Gibbons claimed was the ultimate natural habitat. After descending a steep asphalt road for more than a mile, we entered a humid, overgrown jungle packed with exotic-looking plants. Finally, we'd discovered the wild papayas and mangos Euell had promised, along with a few other main-landers attempting to build grass shacks. They must've read his book, too.

At the end of the rain forest, we discovered a perfect place to camp on an uninhabited sand beach stretching across the gorge between the black rock cliffs that formed the steep valley. In preparation for our descent into the wild, we had purchased one bag of brown rice and two bags of granola to supplement the wild food we planned to harvest. We built a fire on the beach and began preparing our evening meal. In Crete, I had learned that water was an essential ingredient to making rice. But the only water Michael and I could find was in the ocean. Since we knew people often added salt to rice, we boiled ours in pre-salted water conveniently provided by nature. As the sun dropped over the horizon, we prepared our dinner over a blaz-ing bonfire, convinced we'd finally found paradise.

Thirty-six hours later, we were dragging our sweaty, tired bodies up the almost vertical road out of the valley. Our brief so-journ with nature had ended. Seawater rice was inedible. Wild papayas were slimy. Coconut milk was smelly. With nothing else to eat, we polished off our two-week supply of granola in one day and were ready to return to civilization.

The only highlight of our trip around the Big Island was the chance to see Kilauea, the world's most active volcano. Park rangers led Michael, me, and a dozen other curious visitors across acres of jagged black rocks to the edge of a gigantic crater bubbling with red-hot molten lava. As we stood silently inhal-ing sulfur fumes, the volcano belched huge globs of fiery liquid above the height of the rim, almost to our eye level. At the oppo-site end of the crater, the molten rock flowed like a river down the mountain and created a huge cloud of steam as it plunged into the water. In the pre-guardrail era, we were surprised the park rangers led us so close to the edge of the volcano. But we were grateful to get a breathtaking view of raw power shooting up from the center of our planet with enough force to obliterate our ant-like existence.

After three weeks of circling the island of Hawaii without finding anything to do besides bodysurf, sit on the beach, and walk along the melting-hot asphalt roads, we used our AARP island-hopping plane tickets to visit Maui, where we heard magic mushrooms grew wild on every hillside.

Upon arrival, we discovered another important piece of information not found in Gibbons's guidebook—hitchhiking on Maui carried a fine of $500, which exceeded our combined wealth. More experienced transients advised us to stand by the side of the road with our hands at our sides. They said sympathetic drivers, sensing we needed a ride, would stop to give us a lift. We tried that for twelve humid hours before heading back to the airport to cash in our last AARP tickets for a flight to Honolulu.

The luxury hotels and shopping malls lining Waikiki Beach offered little solace to poor travelers like us, but we did make one interesting discovery—a giant yellow tanker docked in the port. Curious about its origins, we questioned a local dockworker, who explained that big ships had no reason to stop in Hawaii, but this one had laid over for engine repairs.

Having always dreamed of working on a "tramp steamer," I asked him if ships ever took on passengers who were willing to work for room and board. He replied that occasionally they did, but the only way to find out was to ask the captain. "The captain is the *only* one who can grant that permission," he proclaimed.

Michael and I cautiously boarded the intimidating vessel in search of the captain's quarters. After wandering through a maze of corridors, we located his cabin and knocked timidly on his door. Seconds later, a bearded Norwegian man in a crisp white uniform opened the door to face two scruffy kids. He politely asked what we wanted and I replied that we were wondering if we could work for our passage on his ship. After a moment's thought, he explained that he was leaving in a few weeks and it would not be appropriate to transfer the ship to a new captain with two young Americans on board. We thanked him for his time and headed back to the dock.

An hour later, over a lunch of fresh pineapple on a nearby street corner, I asked my old friend if he would mind if I returned to the ship and tried again, thinking the captain might be less reluctant if there were only one of us. With his blessing, I took another stroll up the gangway to the same door and the same captain. But this time the answer was different. He explained that since our last visit, one of the crew had fallen ill and was flying back to Norway. Not only would he take me, he would pay me to be a cabin boy. Assuming his answer would be another polite no, I was speechless. After a few seconds, I asked what seemed like a reasonable question.

"When do we leave?"

"At 4:00," he replied.

Calculating that was in three hours, I asked a second question, "Where are we going?"

"Japan," he said.

I pumped his hand with excitement, thanked him repeatedly, and ran off the ship to tell Michael, who was waiting on the dock. I was overwhelmed with emotions. I was ecstatic to be going on an adventure at sea, but scared that I had no idea what I was getting into. I felt guilty for stranding my childhood friend in this godforsaken paradise and anxious about what I had to accomplish in the next three hours.

We caught a bus back up the hill to the youth hostel, where I rolled my extra pair of jeans into my sleeping bag and checked out. Realizing I'd better tell my parents where I was going, I tracked them down on vacation in Florida. Given the time difference, it must have been cocktail hour when they answered the phone, because they seemed deliriously happy that I was taking a Norwegian tanker across the Pacific and wished me a bon voyage.

When we raced back to the dock, the smoke billowing out of the ship's stacks signaled it was ready to go. I said goodbye to Michael and slowly walked up the gangway for the third time. On the open deck, I had no idea what to do. I sat down on my rolled up sleeping bag, leaned against the wall, and looked out over the ship. Noticing it was about as big as a football field, sprouting all kinds of ropes, motors, winches, and other scary mechanical devices, it dawned on me that this job could be dangerous. I remembered that my grandmother's next-door neighbor had joined the Navy, only to be crushed to death by a broken anchor chain. Maybe that would happen to me.

Sailors walked past as I sat staring out over Honolulu Harbor, but no one said a word. I felt very small and alone as the ship pulled slowly away from shore. In the distance, I watched Michael's hand-waving image fade into the afternoon haze. He returned to Maui—where he lived for five more years, learning the art of cultivating cannabis.

I must have barfed a hundred times during my first few days at sea—on the deck, over the side, in the sink, in my sleep, and occasionally in the toilet. The ocean was as smooth as glass as we left Honolulu, but we awoke the next morning to 10-foot waves that tossed the ship, and me, from side to side all day and all night. I bounced off the walls like a pinball as I careened down the hallways. Amused by my landlubbing illness, my Norwegian shipmates advised me to force feed myself until my stomach grew accustomed to the motion. I still wonder whether that was some kind of sailor's practical joke, because the food they served was bad enough to make me sick on dry land. Delicacies like dark brown cheese, fish ball soup, and whale meat went down and came right back up. Eventually, both the sea and my stomach calmed down and I got into the rhythm of the voyage.

Cleaning the cabins of the 35 crewmembers every day was not a difficult task, since the Norwegian mechanics who worked in the engine room were not a particularly fussy bunch. I made their beds, cleaned their sinks, and emptied their garbage while listening to their country music. Since most of them went to sleep covered with grease, they didn't complain if their oil-stained sheets weren't perfectly tucked in.

I found life at sea relaxing. I had my own six-by-ten cabin where I spent my free time reading *Lord of the Rings* and writing in my journal. At night, I wandered the ship watching the moonlit sea glide by. After a few days, I discovered a swimming pool on the upper deck that was the size of an extra-large bathtub. When the weather was warm, I would float in the water watching stars shoot across the night sky. The Norwegians never stopped by.

As a vagabond guest from America, I received special unspoken privileges, like joining the captain as he guided us through the open sea, shouting commands to the engine room. For two weeks, we saw no hint of land, until late one night we arrived in Tokyo. I felt a rush of adrenaline as I stood on the bridge and watched a billion city lights emerge before me as we slid past hundreds of silent ships floating in the harbor.

Arriving in Tokyo was a bit like landing on another planet, inhabited by millions of small people crammed into thousands of small spaces. I joined my Filipino shipmates Speedy, Francisco, and Junior for the Japanese version of bar hopping, which entailed going from one tiny little bar to another only to be waved away by the maître d' with the words "Japanese only." Although I was offended by this apparent discrimination, my shipmates were not easily discouraged and eventually found a place that accepted us. Once inside, seated at a bar that accommodated a dozen (little) people, I understood why we weren't welcomed before. A young Japanese woman stood directly across the bar from every two male customers to pour their drinks, light their cigarettes, and engage them in clever conversation. This intimate ritual proved a little awkward when their customers could barely pronounce *arigato*. Unfazed, we proceeded to visit every bar that would have us, communicating through drunken sign language until it was time to return to the ship.

In addition to Tokyo, we docked at three other ports in Japan—Yokahama, Iwakuni, and Kobe—all big industrial cities with limited attractions to offer the average American visitor. Nonetheless, I ventured into this intense civilization at every opportunity, sometimes with my Filipino shipmates and sometimes by myself, while the Norwegian crew stayed on board playing cards, listening to Merle Haggard, and drinking Ringnes beer.

In each city, I traveled by taxi or subway to the central business district, where I immersed myself in the throngs of Japanese spilling out of stores, restaurants, and pachinko parlors onto the packed sidewalks. I wandered into shops and admired tea sets, watercolors, ivory carvings, and other things for which I had no use. Occasionally I'd buy a postcard. I sipped sake and drank beer with Japanese men who wanted to practice their English until they got too drunk to understand a word. Before midnight I'd board the last tender, which would slip through the gigantic ships to take me home to the security of my cozy cabin with its candles and books.

While we were in Japan, I got a promotion of sorts, from cabin boy to mess man. This change in status was not based on my stellar performance cleaning cabins but rather the result of a Norwegian love triangle. After a week on the ship, I learned that the captain's decision to hire me wasn't based on a crewmember being sent home sick, as he had explained. The previous cabin boy was actually a cabin girl, who had recently married Jon, the ship's mess man. In hindsight, taking their honeymoon cruise with 35 sex-starved Norwegian men was probably a mistake. As Jon confided to me privately, midway through their tour of duty his frisky new wife started fooling around with several of his fellow shipmates. By the time the ship arrived in Honolulu, the captain had decided the situation was out of control and sent her back to Norway—thereby creating a job opening for yours truly. Not surprisingly, Jon was distraught during the long voyage to Japan. When we arrived, he commissioned a white china plate with their wedding picture printed in the center, from one of the floating merchants that surrounded our ship wherever we laid anchor. Jon also received his first communiqué informing him that she wanted a divorce. Faced with the prospect of continuing to serve three meals a day to his wife's lovers and wondering whom she was screwing back at home, he left, leaving me to assume his duties as mess man.

Compared to Japan, Taiwan was more of how I had imagined Asia to be—colorful streets filled with exotic sights, strange smells, and scrambling shoppers buying everything in sight, from bootleg record albums for a quarter to counterfeit English novels for a dime. Having often been the only person on the ship to take shore leave in certain ports, I was surprised to see the entire crew disembarking when we reached Keelung, until I saw the bevy of beautiful Chinese girls on the dock waiting to cling to a sailor all night for a fee of $10.

The primary destination for visiting seamen was a neon-lit street next to the pier that looked like a Wild West movie set featuring establishments like the Hollywood Bar, Long Beach Bar, and Lucky Bar—each filled with young Chinese girls hustling potential customers. The Filipinos and I were the only crewmembers to venture beyond this seedy section of town.

We visited another city in Taiwan called Kaohsiung, where the harbor was filled with ships displaying the flags of dozens of different countries. From my post on the plastic grass by my miniature pool, I watched tug boats pushing cargo ships, fishing boats trying to catch dinner without being crushed, sampans waiting to paddle passengers to shore, and tender boats carrying crews from every continent dressed in their finest attire for a night on the town.

Life on the water provided a strange lens with which to view life on land. For a couple of days after our stop in Taiwan, sex was the only topic of conversation. My fellow crewmembers asked me repeatedly if I had gotten a girl. I responded awkwardly that I didn't have the money, which wasn't true. I guess I could've told them the truth—if I knew what it was.

Next stop was Hong Kong, where I was planning to "pay off" and spend some time visiting with the relatives of a Chinese family who operated the Shing Lee restaurant on Main Street in Evansville, in a building my father owned. However, the day before we arrived, the ship's radio officer informed me that Chinese immigration had denied my visa. Instead of spending the rest of my life in Hong Kong, I spent a day there sharing a feast in a three-story Chinese restaurant that served nothing recognizable to my beef-and-broccoli taste buds, watching ornate furniture being carved by 12-year-old girls (who I'm convinced make everything in China) and sampling my first mango, which didn't taste as good as I'd anticipated. Maybe I should've peeled it first.

We left Hong Kong for Singapore, our last stop and the final leg of my sailing adventure. Heat was the dominant theme of the last few days as we sailed along the coast of Vietnam, the country I had dreaded visiting for so many years. The Navy cruiser bobbing offshore reminded me that the war was still in full swing. My dishwashing job had officially ended, so I had lots of time to float in the pool and ponder the starry sky while wondering about the next chapter of my life. My days and nights on the ship had been so peaceful that I hated to see them end. I finally understood why these merchant seamen preferred a life at sea to the stress of living on land. But I was intrigued about what awaited me in the days ahead as I took a final walk around the deck.

In Singapore, the captain and I both left the ship. I received $370 and a one-sentence letter of recommendation stating that I'd been a satisfactory mess man. After passing through customs, we shook hands and departed in different directions. He was disembarking for a new assignment and I was embarking on new journey. Like most executives, behind his starched suit my captain was just a regular guy who indulged an eager kid who wasn't afraid to ask questions.

Potential outcome if
you don't ask

Potential outcome if
you do ask

Knocking on the captain's door opened a new world for me. Most people my age were graduating from college, beginning their business careers, or heading to graduate school. I was bound for destinations I'd never imagined. Few people are lucky enough to score a paying job on the only tanker stranded on an island in the middle of the ocean, but there are other kinds of "ships" that can transport you to unfamiliar places. You just have to figure out how to ask the captain.

Stalk senior management

My captain was easy to find. Sometimes you have to look a little harder. If someone I want to meet is speaking at a forum, I make sure I'm in the audience. Then I attack the stage afterward. This is not an ideal place to have a conversation, but I introduce myself, get a card, and follow up later. It's also helpful to know where people work out and eat lunch. Inside the office, hallways are great places to get acquainted. Elevators are better, especially on an upper floor. Even the bathroom has potential.

Look for a chance to meet management

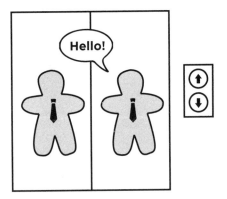

After speaking to a group of students at SMU, Ginger Porter, our Dallas managing director, was headed to the ladies' room when she was approached by a student who was eager to join our firm. In a hurry to reach her destination, Ginger suggested that the young woman walk with her. She used the opportunity to make her case—even after Ginger entered the bathroom stall. Her persistence was rewarded with a paid internship. You only need a few minutes to make a lasting impression no matter where you are.

Social media can be a fertile stalking ground. Twitter delivers business updates, Facebook provides personal insights, and LinkedIn makes connections. But most CEOs don't use social media the way the rest of us do. Usually, public relations people write their posts and tweets. You can follow Mark Zuckerberg on Facebook, but you can't be his friend. The good news is that many lower-profile execs actually type 140 characters by themselves, which makes connecting with them a lot easier. Social media wasn't an option when I was first looking for a job, but today it is a powerful research tool and can be very helpful in building relationships with prospective employers, especially when combined with face-to-face contact.

Recently, I spoke to an auditorium filled with communications majors at Illinois State University about how to create a career. After the presentation, a dozen students approached the stage to introduce themselves and ask questions. One senior seemed genuinely relieved to hear that she had other options in life besides getting a job the day she graduated. Impressed by her confidence, I gave her my card. When I was finished speaking with the others, I took a moment to check my BlackBerry. I was surprised to find an email from the girl I'd just met. She must have written it as she was leaving the building:

> *Hi Mr. Cook! I just wanted to follow up and say thank you for coming to speak to us. This is Angela Ricordati. (I was the second one in line to talk to you. I had the beige jacket on). I was hoping to keep in contact with you, ask for advice, and discuss ANY openings at your company. I would sweep the floors if that were available! You were extremely inspirational and I would love to work with someone with your experience.*

I also noticed that several tweets were posted during my presentation and sure enough, one of them was from Angela. Her approach might seem a little aggressive to some, but not to me. I had just spoken to 200 students and only one seized the opportunity to make a memorable impression on me. It wasn't what she said but how she said it that made an impact. Within five minutes, she had followed up with an email. Even in the business world, few people are this responsive.

After a few more email exchanges, I forwarded her resume to our internship committee, who brought her in for an interview. They reported back that she had interviewed well but other candidates had fared better on the writing test, which is a standard exam that PR firms administer. Based on that limited information, they decided not to offer her an internship, which, I'm sure, was a rational conclusion. Normally, I try not to use my influence to influence their process. But in this case, I am the captain. After thinking about the situation for a couple of days, I asked them to offer her a position, which they did.

I admit this may not seem like a fair way to handle a hiring decision. But life isn't always fair. In Hawaii, I went back to the captain alone and asked to be a cabin boy, leaving my best friend behind. He could've done the same thing, but I was the one who desperately wanted to work on that ship. In the end, the captain chose me.

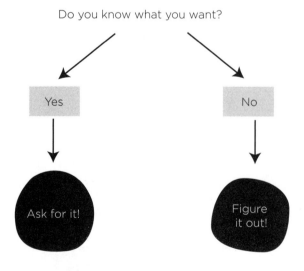

Angela knew what she wanted and wasn't afraid to ask for it. Could any of the other students have done what she did? Of course—but no one else did. She's the type of person I want on my ship. Surprisingly, Angela ended up preferring a career in real estate to PR. Not surprisingly, she still sends me an email every few months.

Prepare an attack

Once I get a shot, I figure I have one chance to hit the target. I start with a little research to determine if I have anything in common with the person I want to impress. Did we grow up in the same town? Do we have any mutual friends? Do we share any interests? These are proven icebreakers and they are easy to discover.

If these connections don't exist, I comment on current events. Was he recently honored with an award I can congratulate him on? Did she just land a big account? Were they featured in an article in my Google Alerts? Ego-building personal questions are surefire winners. How did you get started in this business? How did you become CEO? How did you get to be so brilliant? My strategy is to initiate the conversation with something they care about. Then shift to something I care about.

These initial encounters are a toe in the door. The rest of the foot comes with follow-up. Within 24 hours, before they forget you exist, send an email. Like Angela, remind them of who you are and comment on something they said. Then ask for what you want—a phone call, a meeting, a referral or, if you are feeling particularly cocky, a job. The answer may be no, but the only way to find out is to ask.

Get past no

Since my days as a cabin boy, I have confronted many captains. One was the president of a large consumer products company, whom we hoped would approve a multimillion dollar PR program. Prior to our presentation, the company's director of marketing advised us that his boss was unlikely to comment on our plan unless he really hated a specific idea. If that happened, he instructed us to just simply nod in agreement and move on, believing it would be suicide to try to talk him into something.

Duly intimidated, our jittery team presented a series of PowerPoint slides outlining a dozen separate PR activities for the upcoming holiday season, ranging from retail promotions to story angles for the media. Our favorite idea was a mobile tour featuring a tricked-out vehicle that would showcase the company's newest products to television and radio stations in smaller markets, like Tulsa and Tampa, which they had traditionally ignored. As predicted, the executive sat expressionless as we cheerfully walked through our deck. When we were finished, the only thing he said was, "I don't like the mobile tour."

I was crushed. We had worked for weeks designing the van, mapping out the markets, and researching the media. We were convinced that an aggressive grassroots campaign was the perfect tactic and never anticipated he wouldn't agree. As his staff gathered their papers to exit the conference room, I took a deep breath, looked the president in the eye, and said, "If you only choose one campaign to implement this fall, I would recommend it be the mobile tour."

Everyone in the room turned their attention to their boss, who was not used to being questioned, especially by someone he'd just met. After a moment of awkward silence, he acquiesced with a simple, "Okay." Then got up and left. I'm relieved to report that our mobile marketing tour was a success. In every city, our client's products were featured in so many radio interviews, newspaper stories, and TV broadcasts that we repeated the program for many years.

We were fortunate to have an open-minded client willing to gamble on an unproven idea. Most big organizations have more layers of approval than the Pentagon, and subversive suggestions rarely make it through security. Entrenched middle managers don't climb the corporate ladder by taking chances. They survive by avoiding anything that seems slightly risky. Your job is to sneak past them.

Improvise to get past no

But ignoring your client's advice is tricky. Try not to make a habit of it. There is a thin line between being passionate and being a pest, which I have crossed many times. One of my favorite clients said my middle name is Relentless, which I think is a compliment. But I have learned when to back off.

Going around your direct supervisors can also be dangerous. You won't gain their trust by making suggestions directly to their boss. If you have an idea you believe in, ask for their support in taking it to the next level. If they don't appreciate your thinking or recognize your ability, you need to find someone else who does.

Ultimately, you have to decide how badly you want something. I was dying to work on a ship, which gave me the courage to ask the captain a second time. But if he'd said no, it would've been pointless to ask again. Sending a few emails to your current or prospective employer shows determination. Sending 20 looks more like desperation. If you have a dream worth fighting for, get in the ring. If not, it's better to avoid getting knocked out.

Reply to all

There are safer ways to state your case. I regularly send emails to "all staff" with pronouncements about our business results or progress on key initiatives. I spend hours finding the perfect words to convey just the right message. After 20 rewrites and 5 proofreads, I hit the send button with a deep sense of satisfaction. Then I sit and stare at my computer screen waiting for instant gratification. Nothing appears. I check my sent email to confirm it was delivered. Then I review the address line to make sure it was sent to the right group. Then I examine my computer to see if it is unplugged. Still no response. Has everyone gone home? Are they too busy to read an email? Or did they delete it?

I've just sent what I think is an important email to the entire global staff and no one replies. It's possible my message wasn't as profound as I imagined, but that's not the point. Every employee is missing an opportunity to have a conversation with me about something I'm passionate about, because they're afraid to respond to the captain.

When you get an email from the head of your company, even if you're one of ten thousand on the list—reply!

Hit reply!

Don't just say congratulations or thank you. Even the most powerful executives appreciate honest feedback, and they're the ones that need it most. If you take a few minutes to draft a thoughtful response, it will be noticed. I know from experience, yours may be the only one they get.

Be bold

Every step on the career ladder is about being recognized — for a win, an award, or a phone call. Our company's founder, Al Golin, is a legend because in the beginning of his career, he "asked the captain" when he made a cold call to Ray Kroc, who at the time owned a handful of hamburger restaurants, to see if he needed a PR firm. After six decades of working for McDonald's, Al has created a legacy, but everyone knows the story of that first call. You need to make a similar impression, even if you only have six months. If you want to be a captain tomorrow, you should start by asking one today.

4.

Listen to a Guru

Listening is a critical skill for any senior executive, or anyone who wants to be one, but today it's a lost art. The average talker utters about 16,000 words a day. With the right medication, the average listener's attention span caps out at 27. The result? A lot of missed messages.

The staggering popularity of Facebook and Twitter is based on talking. Talking to anyone or no one. It really doesn't matter. We're a talking society, not a listening one. Or perhaps we're a texting one.

Riding on the bus, sitting in a restaurant, walking down the street, all of us are glued to our mobile phones. Americans aged 18–29 send and receive about 88 text messages a day. Emergency rooms are overflowing with patients who were injured while texting. They're walking into signs, banging into walls, and falling into fountains. Researchers observing pedestrians in Seattle found that one in three people crossing at the city's most dangerous intersections are using a mobile device.

Even without electronic distractions, I've never been a skilled listener. I notice my mind wandering during the shortest conversations, wishing it had a TiVo to rewind to the parts I missed.

But I learned a lesson in India — a place whose spiritual richness and material poorness teaches everyone something profound. Even though I'd grown up without much religious training, I was searching for significance in the birthplace of Jainism, Sikhism, Hinduism, and Buddhism, with a taste of Islam and Christianity mixed in.

After I left Singapore, I spent the next couple of months exploring Southeast Asia, where I lived with a Thai family in Bangkok, swam in the infamous Mekong River in Laos, and watched a dazed dancer rip open a coconut with his teeth in Burma. The only place I skipped was Vietnam, where the war would drag on for three more years.

I'd heard about the perils of Calcutta from eastbound travelers, but like the Grand Canyon, reality defies description. Three words summed it up for me — people, poverty, and heat. Humans were literally everywhere in a city built to hold 150,000 that, at the time, contained more than 5 million. During the day the streets were teeming with people working, hawking, walking, begging, defecating, and dying. Commuters were squirting like Play-Doh through the windows of the multicolored city buses as they dodged scooters, tuk-tuks, rickshaws, and scared cows.

At night, the sidewalks were so jammed with sleeping men, women, and children that pedestrians had to walk in the street to avoid stepping on them. Every inch of ground was a potential living space. A few feet of dirt in front of a government building was home for a family of five Untouchables, living in a makeshift shelter of sheet metal and cardboard tied together with wire and string.

The delayed monsoon season triggered unrelenting heat. At night, my sleep was interrupted by repeated trips down the hall to cool off under a warm shower before returning to a sweat-soaked bed. During the day, I continually quenched my incessant thirst with pineapple and mango lassis, which in turn caused a constant case of dysentery.

Despite all of this, my days in Calcutta were unforgettable. The entire drama of human life played out on the streets every day, gruesome and fascinating at the same time. After a week of wandering through the city, bargaining for trinkets that cost almost nothing, riding in rickshaws powered by emaciated old men, and fending off hundreds of sickly women with crippled children begging for pennies, I decided to head to the mountains. To escape the unrelenting heat, I boarded the Darjeeling Express, which travelled almost as fast as the passengers who walked beside it, to the tea plantations at the base of the tallest mountains in the world.

High in the Himalayas, I met a guru who taught me the secret to listening. One morning, walking alone down Darjeeling's main thoroughfare, I chanced upon a friendly, elderly man with waist-length white hair and beard. He introduced himself as the Hippie Guru of Darjeeling, which seemed fitting since he was wearing the flowing orange robes of a monk. As we walked down a crowded street, he promoted his guru credentials and his mastery of the spiritual world, either trying to impress me or to scam a few rupees. Intent on dazzling him with my own knowledge of Eastern religion, I asked if he'd ever heard of Paul Brunton, an obscure English author of meditation manuals. He immediately replied that he'd read every one of his books. Somewhat incredulous, because I knew Brunton had written more than 20, I sarcastically replied, "You're lying."

The Hippie Guru responded immediately with a hard left hook to my jaw. Stunned by the power of this little old man's blow, I staggered backward, almost losing my balance. Before I could recover, an angry crowd gathered around my attacker, threatening to have him arrested for assault. I tried to intervene, but the fast-growing mob ignored my pleas for mercy. Leaving them screaming in the background, I wandered down the road, wondering whether I had encountered the town nut or had experienced a deep spiritual teaching. I think the answer is both.

Regardless of his mental capacity, the Hippie Guru of Darjeeling taught me a valuable lesson. Sometimes you should just **SHUT UP!**

If you're not talking or texting, a miraculous thing happens — you actually hear what the other person is saying. I might have discovered the meaning of life, if I wasn't so busy mouthing off.

Ask questions

Starting out in a new job is like being a novice monk. You're an empty vessel with little knowledge of the industry, the company, and sometimes yourself. Your mission is to fill that vessel as quickly as you can. The best way to do that is to ask questions.

Whoever invented questions was brilliant, because you don't have to know anything to ask a question. You just need to overcome your fear of sounding stupid. If it helps, you can even begin your question by saying, "This is a dumb question." I do that all the time, because questions help me listen. When you listen you learn. When you learn, you get smart.

Asking a question is the best way to learn something new!

Instead of calling the Hippie Guru a liar, I should've asked him a question: "What is your favorite book?" "Do you believe in reincarnation?" "What is the secret to success?" Maybe I would have gained more than a sore jaw.

I'm not an authority on anything. I can't expound on any topic for more than a few minutes, but I can ask questions all day long. Perfecting the art takes practice. Before meeting a potential employer or an important client, write down 10 questions that demonstrate your knowledge of their business. Questions that convince them you can solve their problems. Questions they may be asking themselves. Questions that will make them remember you. You're more interesting to others when you talk about things they're already interested in.

Voltaire said it best: "Judge a man by his questions, not his answers."

Listen between the lines

My second listening guru was Heinz Wandtke, who shared my Calcutta hotel room at the infamous dollar-per-night Modern Lodge, which was anything but. On the surface, Heinz was *typisch Deutsch*, with a round face and short hair neatly parted to one side. A naïve 28-year-old who'd grown up in a small farming village, he'd arrived in Southeast Asia speaking only German. Unlike his fellow travelers, Heinz drank beer, ate blood sausage (in places where most people were afraid to eat anything), and even hired Indian prostitutes, who begged him for baksheesh throughout his brief encounters.

In our sparsely furnished cell, Heinz shared tales of his past under the glow of a bare light bulb hanging from the ceiling. He'd begin speaking in thick but understandable English. Then, after a few minutes of conversation, he'd gradually shift to German. I would listen for a while, not comprehending a word, before mentioning that I didn't understand. Nudged from his altered state of consciousness, he'd quickly apologize and begin again in English, then morph into German until I again reminded him that I *nicht sprechen Deutsch*. After an hour or so, I would give up and listen attentively for the rest of the evening.

Carrying on a conversation with someone speaking a different language is an effective way to hone your listening skills. You have to focus on every word and scrutinize every gesture to understand the context of what is being communicated. Then you respond slowly and carefully to make sure the other person understands your reply.

In any language, Heinz is a master storyteller whose tales are filled with intricate details about his childhood, his neighbors, and his dreams. Listening to him is a workout for my ears and my brain because it requires a level of concentration that I rarely achieve in other conversations. Staying a few days with him in his modest Bremen apartment is like spending a week in an expensive yoga retreat.

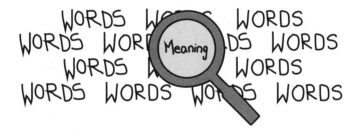

Whether on the phone or in person, today I deal with many people who speak English as a second language. Thanks to Heinz, I can better understand the meaning behind their words. You can practice this technique by tuning into telenovelas on Univision or by watching Bollywood classics on iTunes. If you really concentrate on what people are saying and how they're saying it, you'll be surprised how much you can understand in any language.

Put away your phone

Heinz is also a gifted listener. He isn't distracted by a mobile phone or tablet, because he doesn't own one. For most of his life, his only source of news was a scratchy transistor radio. I believe this has nurtured his creative depth. He marvels at the structure of a flower like he's never seen one before. He will sit for hours and watch a sunset. He draws intricate portraits of his own dreams. Every artist and musician knows that improvising begins with listening.

Unlike Heinz, most of us are addicted to multitasking. *AdAge* magazine estimates that in the evening, after school and work, Millennials might switch "information channels" 28 times an hour, bouncing from TV, YouTube, Twitter, and texting to iTunes, Pinterest, Farmville, and Facebook.

Millenials switch
information channels

28 times per hour

My family of four owns six TVs, five laptops, five iPods, four iPads, three desktop computers, three iPhones, three Wiis, two WiiUs, two BlackBerries, one Kindle, one Xbox, one Nintendo

3DS, and 50 chargers. We're not the typical American household (which owns only 24 devices), but you get the idea. No one is paying attention.

The same is true at work. At meetings I lead, people are constantly playing with devices. From the front of the room, it is hard to tell whether they're tweeting my brilliant comments or playing Words With Friends. The only thing I know for sure is they aren't listening to me—even though they think they are. Studies show people believe their brains can do two things at once without compromising their ability. But experiments have proven that listening comprehension drops 30 percent when you are typing or texting. If you want to test this theory, direct a question to someone who is tapping out a message; they will respond like a deer in the LED lights.

If you are always on your phone...

you might miss all the amazing
things right in front of you

To ensure he has everyone's undivided attention at cabinet meetings, President Obama insists the participants mark their phones with Post-it Notes and drop them in a basket. These are the men and women running the country. If they can live without email for an hour, so can you.

If you're in an interview, turn off your phone. If you're in a meeting, leave it in your pocket or your purse. No one, except Heinz, can resist the temptation of a device sitting in plain sight. Whether you are having a conversation with your boss, your client, your assistant, your friends, your kids, or your dog, don't check for messages. Picking up your phone is a direct signal that you don't care what they're saying. The Hippie Guru would punch you in the nose.

Write and repeat

A pen and a piece of paper are the only devices that really say, "I'm listening." The simple fact that you bring them to a meeting suggests you value the other person's ideas enough to write them down, even if you toss your notes in the trash when you get back to your desk. I worked for several years with a well-regarded, senior-level executive who came to every meeting empty handed. Maybe he had a photographic memory, but sitting with his hands folded while clients explained their problems seemed to say, "I don't really give a shit." Not surprisingly, he didn't last long with us—or anyone else—because his suit was as empty as his hands.

When someone says something important, write it down. If it's really important, underline it. If it's super important, put a star next to it. If it's the most brilliant thing you have ever heard, draw a box around it. This is how you listen with your hands. I know you think you can probably take better notes on your laptop. But remember, the person in front of you has no idea if you are typing their comments or updating your Facebook page. If paper feels too old fashioned, try Noteshelf on your iPad.

When you hear something
important, write it down

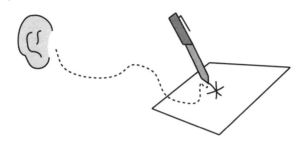

Repeating what someone says also proves you're listening and helps clarify what the speaker wants you to do. Like many busy executives, I'm lousy at giving direction. I speak in shorthand, expecting others to fill in the blanks. If they don't ask questions, there's a 50 percent chance they'll misunderstand me. It's usually my fault, but unfortunately, it becomes their problem.

The same is true with our clients. They give us elaborate written briefs, but when we repeat what we think they told us, we often discover they want something completely different. We make a practice of checking in with them halfway through the planning process to share our preliminary thinking, which helps us stay on track and proves we're listening. No matter how small the task, writing it down—and repeating it—dramatically increases the probability you'll get it right.

Prevent politics

In a typical office, people talk a lot. Unfortunately, their favorite topic of conversation is what's wrong with everybody else. All day long, people criticize their bosses, coworkers, customers, clients, and even their agencies. This unproductive banter creates a toxic culture and a lack of trust. Don't join in, even if everyone around you does.

Office politics are unavoidable, but to minimize them we hired another guru, who began as our receptionist and is now our executive coach. Daniel Pitlik is a professional listener. He helps us resolve interpersonal issues that have a negative impact on our culture. We pay him a monthly retainer to mediate rocky relationships, motivate junior staff, and counsel senior executives. We can tell him anything, no matter how sensitive. Because Daniel never gossips about others, we know he won't gossip about us.

Starting out, Daniel was enlightened by the idea that listening is the most valuable human skill. It had never really occurred to him that listening was more important than thinking, speaking, or doing. Putting that philosophy into practice, Daniel found that listening made him a better consultant, a better boyfriend, and a better human being. "Too many think listening is waiting for their turn to talk," he says.

Sometimes being a CEO is like being a therapist. Every day, staff members stop by my desk (I don't have an office) to explain their problems and ask for advice. Sometimes the issues are work related. Sometimes they are personal. I can only help if I'm truly listening to what they're saying and how they're feeling. Whether their issues are trivial or critical, I try to understand them. When I can't, I call Daniel.

When you are just starting a new job, try to tune in to what is happening in your work environment. Learn how decisions are made and who is making them. Understand who is on the way up and on the way out. But when you're in the office, don't gossip about your coworkers or complain about your boss. Even if they're true, negative comments ultimately make you look bad.

If you need to vent, find a guru like Daniel, who you can trust. Or better yet, become a guru yourself. Listening confidentially to your coworkers' problems, even if you can't solve them, is critical to any career.

Avoid arguments

One of my early clients invented the world's first french fry vending machine. He was a stiff-upper-lipped British gentleman who concocted the idea for his innovative device in the aftermath of triple-bypass surgery. According to his heartwarming story, seeing all the various tubes coming in and out of his body in the intensive care ward inspired the patented technology for cooking extruded potatoes in hot grease.

Despite my best efforts, this aristocratic entrepreneur and I didn't see eye-to-eye on the future of french fries, the name of the product, or the time of day. After suffering through a dozen heated discussions with me, he finally told the owner of my firm, "If this imbecile doesn't shut up, I am going to spit blood!"

Not surprisingly, I was taken off the account. Given the circumstances, this may seem like a reprieve, but no one likes to be told they don't measure up, even if they dislike the person telling them. In the long run, my career has been more successful than his, but I learned that it doesn't pay to fight about every single thing, especially with the people who are paying your bills.

How persuasive your approach is

In business, there's no such thing as winning an argument. The best you can hope for is a compromise that everyone can live with. Listening is how you get there. Even if you violently disagree with the other person's opinion, listen and acknowledge it. Then suggest a revision to their idea by asking the question, "What if…?" Improving on someone else's idea is always more persuasive than rejecting it.

Say something

Being a good listener doesn't mean being a wallflower. If you sit through an entire meeting without saying a word, people will question why you were there. Everyone needs to make a contribution, even if it's just a couple of smart questions. If you're unsure of yourself or uncomfortable with the topic, plan questions in advance and wait for just the right moment to ask them. As Eminem says, "You only get one shot. Do not miss your chance to improvise."

There are times when you need to assert your opinions and times when it's better to shut up. The next time you're tempted to interrupt one of your coworkers, bosses, or clients, consult your inner guru. You may avoid getting punched in the mouth.

5.

Enlist an Entourage

I've met a lot of famous people. But I'm friends with many more people who've tried to become famous and never made it. What's the difference between these two groups? There are the usual answers like talent, beauty, brains, and persistence. The truth is, behind all famous people there are teams of highly paid professionals dedicated to keeping them in the spotlight.

Don't be fooled by legends like Mark Zuckerberg, who showed up on Wall Street wearing a hoodie to launch his IPO. While his unassuming persona may be appealing, behind the scenes Zuckerberg has legions of well-heeled brokers, lawyers, and investment bankers working hard to keep Facebook's stock from falling off the charts. If you want to be a billionaire, a senator, or a rock star, you need to enlist an entourage that is going to devote every waking hour to making you look good.

Throughout my career, I've focused on making other people famous, beginning with Caroline Peyton. After three years of wandering around the world, I'd returned to finish my final year of college in Bloomington, where I met the lead singer of a band called the Screaming Gypsy Bandits performing at a rundown

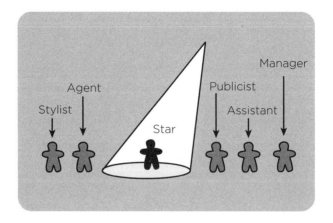

train station converted into a bar. After many late nights at the Depot, I became her boyfriend and eventually her manager, which meant I was the primary person responsible for her future success.

My first step on her road to stardom was managing a fledgling music company called Bar-B-Q Records, which was formed by Caroline's musical partner and producer, Mark Bingham. Working in a windowless basement office, I was responsible for securing funding to produce our homegrown albums and figuring out how to sell them.

The music scene in Bloomington was thriving in the seventies. Indiana University had the largest music school in the country, which sustained a community of music students and professional musicians. Some of these became quite well known, such as John Mellencamp—a slick rock-star-to-be, who at the time went by Johnny Cougar. Launched in Australia by David Bowie's entourage, Mellencamp waited until his career was well established before he dropped his stage name and acknowledged his small-town roots in nearby Seymour, Indiana. John Hiatt was a more serious songwriter who'd recorded a moderately successful album and played on the Indianapolis club circuit.

In total, Bar-B-Q Records released eight albums on a shoestring budget. Our two biggest-selling artists were Bill Wilson, a hard-working singer/songwriter, and Caroline, who sang complex Bach cantatas, corny country standards, and full-on rock and roll.

To spread the word about Bar-B-Q, I tried to persuade music reviewers around the country to write positive reviews of our records. Being a publicist wasn't too difficult, because, despite being recorded in a converted garage, our records were just as good as the ones coming out of LA and New York. But if people read about our music, in those pre-Internet days, they had no way to hear it. To solve that problem, I promoted our albums to all the major-market radio stations and pestered them daily to play a cut or two. Because program directors were reluctant to broadcast music unless their listeners could buy it, I attempted to convince indifferent regional distributors to place our albums in local record stores.

As Caroline's agent, I tried to expand her notoriety by booking gigs around the Midwest at small clubs willing to hire unknown talent. Every weekend, I became a roadie and drove her and her band to Indianapolis, Terre Haute, or West Lafayette, where I operated the sound system that I strapped to the roof of the car. After five sets, I would pack up the equipment and drive home with enough money to pay the $100 monthly mortgage on our cabin in the Brown County woods.

After a few fun but frustrating years, I realized it was futile to be doing management, publicity, promotion, distribution, and representation all by myself. We needed help from the music wizards who were experts at making people famous.

To find them, we travelled the yellow brick road to California, where Caroline played one-week stints at The Boarding House in San Francisco and the once-famous Troubadour in Los Angeles, where in better days Elton John had made his US debut. We were still excited to meet the legendary owner, Doug Weston, who was impressed enough with Caroline to suggest we move to LA. We took his advice and drove 2,000 miles back to Indiana, rented our cabin, said goodbye to our friends, packed our possessions into a U-Haul trailer, and drove back to the Emerald City with our dog, Aretha.

Moving from Bloomington, Indiana to Los Angeles, California would be an entertaining premise for a reality show. As the main contestants, we were the real-life version of the Beverly Hillbillies, except we lived a long way from Beverly Hills. Our quaint little cottage on Mount Washington was only slightly larger than my house on Crete. Surrounded by redwood decks and a small yard filled with fruit trees, our cozy aviary was not at all what we'd expected in this sprawling metropolis. Our next-door neighbor had a pen full of chickens, which made us feel right at home. There was even a miniature potbelly stove in the living room, although the weather was rarely cold enough to use it.

The biggest contrast in our new lifestyle was a complete lack of income. In the Midwest, we earned a reasonable living playing clubs on the weekends, but in LA the financial dynamics of the music scene were curiously reversed. Every venue was an "industry showcase," which meant bands marketed their own appearances, and solicited their friends to buy tickets, while the club owners kept the money. The economics of this system meant that after most gigs, each band member cleared almost enough cash to pay his bar tab. Despite the lack of monetary reward, hundreds of musicians competed for slots on the bill of seedy rock clubs like Madame Wong's, Gazzarri's, the Whiskey, the Roxy, and, of course, the Troubadour. As our income declined and our nest egg disappeared, I worked for tips.

Three years into our LA story, we'd played every club 100 times, called every record label 50 times, made a dozen demo tapes, and met every fly-by-night producer, including a 350-pound man who claimed he'd discovered The Monkees. Caroline dubbed vocals for Pia Zadora and taught Toni Basil how to sing "Mickey." She even won the world's first reality program — *The Gong Show*. However, major record labels weren't interested in the next Bonnie Raitt. They were trying to catch a newer wave, led by a popular local band called The Knack, who later became a one-hit wonder with "My Sharona."

Our lack of success taught me an important lesson. People rarely become stars on their own, no matter how talented they are. We did our best to gain entrance to the Hollywood scene, but like many other hopefuls who travel there from small towns across America, we were never able to open the right doors.

Ironically, Caroline's first and only break in Tinsel Town came in a Broadway musical. While she was busy not getting famous in Los Angeles, Linda Ronstadt was getting even more famous in New York as the star of *The Pirates of Penzance*. The New York Shakespeare Festival's updated version of Gilbert and Sullivan's light opera had become the hot ticket of the season, costarring newcomer Kevin Kline as the Pirate King. Our Hoosier friend Mike Connors, who had been Kevin's struggling-actor roommate in Manhattan, arranged for Caroline to audition for the show's touring company, which was about to premiere in Los Angeles.

The show's director was so impressed with Caroline's performance that he selected her to play Edith, the oldest of the seven sisters. More importantly, he assigned her to be the understudy for Linda Ronstadt's character, Mabel, who was to be played by Pam Dawber, of *Mork and Mindy* fame, alongside a not-yet-famous Barry Bostwick as the Pirate King and pop star Andy Gibb as Frederic. We were blown away by the possibilities, not to mention the $600-per-week salary.

After a month of rehearsal, *Pirates* opened to rave reviews at the Ahmanson Theatre, two blocks from where yours truly was working as a doorman at the Biltmore Hotel. The opening performance was followed by a huge celebration for the city's cultural elite in the Music Center's elegant ballroom with ice carvings, mountains of shrimp, tuxedoed classical musicians, and two bug-eyed Hoosier transplants. Caroline got so drunk that she threw up on the way home.

The following weekend, Caroline called the house phone attached to the front of the hotel to tell me that she would be taking Pam Dawber's place in the sold-out evening performance because Dawber had lost her voice. Since the show had just opened, Caroline had focused solely on learning her part and had not yet rehearsed the lead role. She was more terrified than thrilled.

Equally anxious, I informed the head bellman that I had an emergency at home, tossed my doorman's uniform into my locker, and raced up Bunker Hill to the theater. I still remember the sick-with-excitement feeling gripping my stomach as I stood in the sound booth at the back of the elegant auditorium, wearing jeans and the white shirt with cut-off sleeves that I wore under my doorman costume. Before the show began, the announcer dutifully informed the audience that Pam Dawber, whom everyone had waited months to see, would be replaced by Caroline Peyton, whom no one had ever heard of. The disappointed crowd moaned and booed.

Although she missed a few of her marks, her voice was powerful and perfect. The audience realized they had witnessed something special as they stood and cheered for what seemed like an hour at the end of the show. The loudest clapping came from the very back of the theater.

The show played for three months and despite the best doctors and vocal coaches in the country, Dawber missed many of her performances, which meant Caroline regularly stepped into her shoes. Each time, the audience groaned at the beginning but roared at the end.

When the show left Los Angeles, the director asked Caroline to assume the starring role for a one-year tour, alongside Jim Belushi, who was then only known as John's brother, and Peter Noone, formerly the lead singer of Herman's Hermits. They tripled her salary and her billing. Her career was finally taking off, while mine was crash-landing.

I was proud, excited, and unemployed. The New York Shakespeare Festival didn't need me to book venues, peddle records, arrange interviews, or operate the sound system. They had a hundred more qualified professionals to do all that. Caroline finally had her entourage. I just wasn't part of it.

Despite our limited success, Caroline and I had been partners in her career from the beginning. For the first time, I was just a groupie with nothing much to do but sit around and watch. Before she left on tour, we sat at our kitchen table overlooking the lights of Echo Park and talked about our future. We agreed this was the opportunity we had both worked toward for a long time, but we also acknowledged that being separated for much of the coming year was going to be tough. We knew, but didn't want to face, the reality of what that meant.

The music business taught me that if I ever wanted to be successful, I was going to need a lot of help. Without the continuous involvement of my friends, family, and colleagues, I would never have become a CEO. No matter how talented you are, you're always going to be competing with people who have more

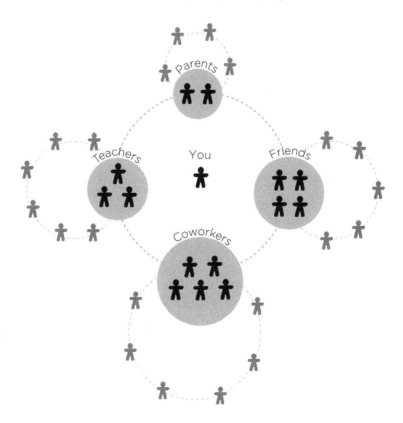

experience and better connections. Scaling the career cliff all by yourself is admirable, but not advisable. If you really want to get to the top, you need to start recruiting your entourage now.

Leverage your parents

In the beginning, your family will be the most likely people to help you out. Your parents can introduce you to their friends in the business world, who in turn can introduce you to prospective employers. Don't be embarrassed to leverage their connections. Every week I get a resume from a business colleague recommending the son or daughter of a friend. They always get interviewed and sometimes they get hired.

Exploit your teachers

Your teachers can also be effective advocates. I pay attention to passionate recommendations from college professors. Even if you are C student, most teachers are happy to help out, and many are well connected in their fields of study. Ask them to forward your resume with a flattering cover note. The same goes for guest lecturers. They come to campus because they want to help students entering their profession. Never let them leave without getting a business card.

Access your alumni

No matter how small or obscure, every school has successful alumni who take pride in their alma mater (and their fraternities or sororities). They may be total strangers to you, but you have a connection that is meaningful to them, even if they graduated years ago. With a little research you can find the alumni who are established in your chosen field. If you can, get an introduction from a school official who knows them. If not, track them down on your own and send an email establishing your connection and asking for help. Many prominent professionals feel a deep sense of gratitude to the institutions that enabled their prosperity. Exploit it.

Scott Farrell, the president of our corporate practice, returns once a year to speak at his alma mater, the University of Wisconsin. He even holds office hours on campus to review resumes and offer career advice, because he believes his professors were instrumental in his career. After every lecture, he tells the students he will never turn down a Badger who wants an informational interview or help networking. His only regret is that more students don't take him up on the offer.

Tap into your friends

You should also get a little help from your friends. When I made the decision to pursue a career in PR, the first person I recruited was my pal Eric Monson, a graphic designer who was semi-famous for his iconic Tony Alva skateboard ads. Eric worked for several prestigious clients from his Century City studio, but every time I began a new venture, he would design my collateral for free.

You'll need a designer to lay out your resume, a writer to edit your cover letter, a coach to prepare you for interviews, a stylist to make you look professional, a producer to film your video, a photographer to take your picture, a community manager to build your online profile, and maybe even a trainer to keep you in shape. Your network of friends can provide many of these services, and most will do it for free because they want the experience and may need your help someday.

Your friends can also introduce you to their friends who have budding careers, and who can refer you to a broader range of opportunities. My first shot at a grown-up job came through a friend of a friend of a friend of a friend. It pays to have as many as you can. You may be six degrees from Kevin Bacon, but you're probably only two or three from a good job.

You can also supplement your entourage on the Internet. There are dozens of sites that can improve your employability by designing your resume or composing a cover letter. If you are wondering what to say in an interview, you can practice Q&A

on YouTube. If you need help deciding what to wear, you can Google the perfect wardrobe.

Nurture a network

Most people already have the beginnings of an entourage and don't even know it. Make a list of all the people you know through school, work, sports, friends, and family. Then mentally assign each of them a role on your team. You'll be surprised how much support you can enlist. This may sound like a self-serving exercise, but I know from experience you're going to need help.

Populate your entourage with people you encounter in your job search. During every interview ask, "Is there is anyone else you suggest I contact?" Don't leave without a new name to add to your list.

As your entourage multiplies, apprise them of your progress. When you finally land a new job, thank them for their help. Don't stop once you're employed. Keep in touch with everyone you meet. You may need them to land your next job. Your entourage will support you forever, if you do the same for them.

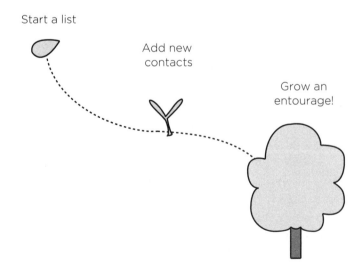

Nurture your network

Start a list

Add new contacts

Grow an entourage!

Choose a champion

Lots of companies have mentorship programs that assign existing staff to help new recruits adapt to the corporate environment by taking them out to lunch and giving them advice. Mentors are nice. Everyone should have one.

But what you really need is a champion. A champion is a mentor on steroids. Someone who recognizes your talents, promotes you to others, lobbies for you to get more money, and defends you when you make a mistake.

How do you choose a champion? Usually, they choose you. Your job is to make that easy. The process begins by getting the attention of the senior staff at your company. Once you're noticed by someone you can trust, begin to cultivate that relationship by seeking counsel on difficult issues, gaining insight on other executives, probing for new opportunities, and simply spending time with him or her.

Al Golin, the founder of our firm, is the closest thing I've ever had to a role model. His self-deprecating, Midwestern charm reminds me of my father (though Al hates to hear that because he looks more like my brother). He's 80 percent wise old sage and 20 percent grumpy old man. I hope to achieve that balance myself someday.

In his 80s, Al still comes into work every day. Unlike those who retire to "spend more time with their family," he claims he works so he doesn't have to. He loves to read the newspaper, but throws it under his desk when I walk up to be sure I don't think he's goofing off. He hates change, but when it happens, he embraces it better than anyone. When we moved to an open space plan, Al happily gave up his office but insisted on keeping his 30-year-old chair.

I've been lucky to have Al as my champion. He's supported the decisions I've made, even if he didn't agree with them. He tells the staff that I'm doing a good job when they may not think so. He even speaks highly of me to my in-laws, who actually believe him.

Everybody needs an Al. Someone who will support you at work, no matter how badly you screw up. Someone who will threaten to quit if anyone threatens to fire you. Someone who reminds you of a parent, but gets mad when you say so.

Build a team

Getting a job is like running for president. As a candidate, you need an aggressive marketing team to help you win. Once you're elected, you need a loyal management team to ensure you survive, because the average office contains just as much politics as the Oval one.

Assemble your team

When I was promoted to president of GolinHarris, I moved from the LA office, where I was beloved, to our headquarters in Chicago, where I was unknown. The day before I arrived, the senior people in the company lined up outside the CEO's office to lobby against reporting to me. They didn't dislike me. They just weren't part of my entourage.

My first year was tough. I mostly worked alone on uninspiring projects that I invented, like writing my own job description. I remember asking one senior vice president when she could introduce me to her client. Her response was, "Why would I ever do that?" Another colleague, with a big belly and white beard, sued me for saying he looked like Santa Claus—when he was standing in front of a Christmas tree.

While I was rethinking the wisdom of my move, work began to improve. I sought out others' input and engaged them in new initiatives. I asked about their frustrations, their ambitions, and their personal lives. Gradually, they realized I was there to help them, not just myself. I'm proud that more than ten years later, despite massive changes in our company, I'm still working with the same team of executives. They're responsible for my success.

Starting every new job means building a new entourage. Choose the people you think will always be loyal. Cultivate their trust with interesting assignments and new opportunities. Coach them when they need help and encourage them when they don't. In the beginning, your crew may only be one or two. As your responsibilities grow, recruit new troops. By the time you're CEO, you may have a whole army.

Don't lose touch

I'm a small-time CEO, which means I have a small entourage. My assistant schedules my appointments and books my travel. Our community manager helps with my tweets and posts. Our marketing director books my interviews and speaking engagements. A retired policeman drives me to the airport. And my wife picks out my suits. Despite their help, I'm not famous. There is another level.

Superstar CEOs are the royalty of the business world, ruling over massive empires. As the CEO of the Walt Disney Company, Michael Eisner was in that elite class. His handlers wrote his speeches, managed his schedule, rehearsed his interviews, guarded his body, designed his wardrobe, and literally rolled out the red carpet everywhere he went.

GolinHarris worked for five different Disney divisions and I helped organize several major events for Mr. Eisner, but never actually met him because I couldn't get past his entourage.

Even so, I learned more about Image making from Disney than they did from us. We were honored to land the assignment to launch a new billion-dollar theme park called Disney California Adventure. For this project, Eisner's team included hundreds of people who worked for six months to orchestrate every detail of a two-hour event that began with a brief speech and ribbon cutting before a horde of international media. In the beginning, the park was a flop, but on that sunny Southern California morning, his entourage reminded the world that Michael Eisner was King of the Magic Kingdom.

Big-time CEOs live in a rarefied atmosphere, unlike the world inhabited by their employees and their customers. You just have to look at annual salary surveys to realize that the heads of America's biggest companies aren't worried about paying their rent. Many of them grew up with money, attended the finest private schools, and socialized with people just like them. But cultural elitism can be dangerous in the 21st century's emerging, multicultural economy, where every bigwig needs to know how the "small people" live.

Tony Hayward, the former CEO of BP, set the standard for being out of touch. He had a stellar track record for growing his company's share price, but he'd built no equity with the general public. His aristocratic British lifestyle was at odds with the victims of the crisis his company caused. His mannerisms and language emphasized that gulf every time he spoke to the press or went sailing on his yacht. Finally, he "got his life back," but not until he did as much damage to BP's reputation as the oil spill. Even the best PR teams can't always keep an executive from putting his Ferragamos in his mouth.

Keep old friends and everyday people in your entourage. No matter how successful you become, they're always happy to remind you that you're still just a dumb Hoosier. My mother used to brag to her friends that I was a CEO, until my brother asked her if she knew what that meant. She had no idea.

I'm in the image business. People employ my agency to make their products, their companies, and themselves look good. We're responsible for minimizing their weaknesses and emphasizing their strengths. This is help everyone needs.

Someday you may be able to afford a PR firm to polish your brand, but until that time you need to leverage your family, friends and coworkers to make you shine.

6.

Work for Tips

This year, 85 percent of the 3.2 million US students who graduate from college will move back home, and 22 percent won't be able to get a job. Of those who are able to find employment, more than 50 percent will work as waitresses and baristas. If you're one of them, you're lucky.

Customer service is the heart of business. If an executive doesn't understand what is required to keep his customers happy, he will fail. Nowhere is this truer than in the hospitality industry, where gratifying guests has become a science. Car dealers and department stores have studied the practices of the Four Seasons to learn the secrets of their world-renowned service. Every CEO should be required to work for tips.

Like most people pursuing a career in the entertainment industry, I had to find a way to support myself. My first paying job in the City of Angels was working as a paperboy. Instead of tossing newspapers from a bicycle onto people's porches, I hauled bundles of the *Los Angeles Times* in my Chevy Suburban and stuffed them in the metal dispensers on downtown street corners. Not seeing a bright future in newspaper distribution, I

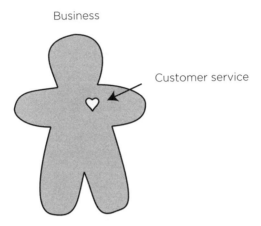

Business

Customer service

decided to stop by the four-star Biltmore Hotel, which I passed every day on my paper route.

There I met the British concierge Bob Duncan, who sported an artificial orange suntan, a dainty three-finger handshake, and claimed to have been a roadie for the Beatles. Coincidentally, one of his four doormen was retiring that week after 25 years on the job. Exaggerating my charm and hospitality experience, I convinced Mr. Duncan (he insisted we call him that) to offer me a job on the spot. Two days later, I was standing on Olive Street under the stately portico of an historical landmark wearing a black top hat and grey tails, politely welcoming guests to the hotel.

Being a doorman was the best job ever. I worked four nights a week in the congenial Southern California weather, checked in thousands of eccentric guests, parked hundreds of expensive cars, and befriended dozens of street people, while pocketing about 80 tax-free dollars a day. And I learned a valuable lesson—the secret to customer service is the little things.

Name names

Remembering people's names is a little thing and I'm terrible at it. But Sammy, a veteran of the Biltmore front door, taught me a trick—luggage tags. When a car pulled up in front of the hotel, our job was to open the car door with an enthusiastic "Welcome to the Biltmore!" and then ask if they were checking in. If the reply was yes, we immediately popped their trunk and loaded their luggage onto a baggage cart. As the guests disappeared into the hotel, we glanced at their luggage tags and memorized their names.

This information became critical in the next phase of the process. Doormen are the undisputed rulers of the front of the hotel, but that domain is limited. Once we pass through the front door, we enter the realm of money-hungry bellmen, who ply guests with valuable information about ice machines and television remotes while putting away their bags. Who couldn't get a $5 tip after all that? We had to be much more creative when we escorted our clients from the curb to the front desk. Before we turned to exit the building, we would politely say, "Thank you Mr. 'Whatever It Said on Your Luggage Tag.' I hope you enjoy your stay with us."

Even in the confusion of gathering their belongings, finding their credit cards, and controlling their kids, the sound of their name reminded them that I had just lugged five heavy suitcases from their car. Only then did they dip into their pockets for a couple of bills to hand to me.

If you're working for tips, develop your own tricks to remember people's names. Credit cards are the luggage tags of the restaurant industry, but they don't come out until the end. Reservations are a good way to learn the identity of at least one member of the party. You can also start by telling the customers your name and see if they respond in kind. The serious payoff comes when you remember returning guests. That makes them feel really important.

The Beverly Hills Hotel was famous for hosting big names like Frank Sinatra, Marilyn Monroe, and Howard Hughes.

When I worked there, the property had lost some of its shine, but the staff treated every guest like a star, starting behind the front desk, where the manager posted head shots and press clippings of the guests scheduled to arrive that day. Every member of the team memorized the faces to be certain they greeted their celebrity clientele by name.

The same was true at the legendary Polo Lounge, where the 40-year veteran maître d' knew the names of every Hollywood producer, director, and star. One of Hollywood's most respected power brokers, Nino Osti was responsible for orchestrating the well-established seating hierarchy, dominated by three green-leather booths visible to everyone. If Nino allowed you to have lunch at one of those tables, you were Hollywood royalty. He relegated everyone else to the back room.

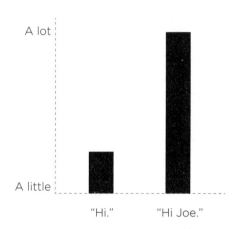

How important Joe feels

While catering to big egos might seem irrelevant to ordinary humans, there is a simple lesson to be learned. People feel important when you remember who they are. When I call a hotel operator to ask for a wake-up call, I'm impressed when they read my name from their computer screen. I feel the same way when a flight attendant recognizes me, or my neighborhood barista knows I want a grande nonfat cappuccino.

Here are a few other valuable tidbits to know about people — birthdays, hometowns, alma maters, teams, wines, hobbies, workouts, and anything about their kids. While these may seem obvious, personal connections are the foundation of business relationships. It took me three months to get a meeting with the CEO of one of the nation's largest insurance companies. In preparation for my audience in his walnut-paneled office, I read his bio, his speeches, and every article about him. Before I could mention the information I'd accumulated, he said, "I understand you used to live in LA." He too had done his homework, or had someone do it for him. In any case, I was impressed that this big-time executive had bothered to find out anything about his company's new PR guy. Maybe he'd worked for tips.

Name badges are the luggage tags of the business world. I wish people wore them every day. But even when they do, it's obvious when you glance down to read them. Business cards help in a first encounter, but after that you have to rely on other tricks. Ideally, you can get a list of the people attending a meeting beforehand. If possible, get pictures to go with the names and study them in advance. For large meetings, make sure you also know who is on your team. Nothing is more embarrassing than introducing yourself to your coworkers.

Pay attention to these!

If you have developed a good memory, you're way ahead of me. If you haven't, use your tipping job to practice. Remembering people's names is a little thing that makes a big impression.

Sweat the details

When my daughter Emily was an intern at the Four Seasons Hotel in Chicago, she learned to smile and greet guests exactly ten feet before meeting them in the hallway. When people asked for directions, she was trained not to point the way, but to stop whatever she was doing and walk them to their destination. It's no coincidence that I've seen these same friendly gestures repeated at hotels around the world. These are the little things people remember. Howard Schultz did.

Before he was one of the world's most famous CEOs, Howard visited our LA office. He was opening his first Starbucks in California and needed a PR agency to help build awareness for a brand that few outside of Seattle had ever heard of. After a little research, we figured his upstart company had potential and decided to impress him.

My business partner, Maureen Crow, had a flair for details. In this case, she wanted to serve Howard a simple cup of coffee — his coffee. Because you couldn't buy Starbucks anywhere outside of Seattle, we called the company headquarters, which shipped a bag of beans to our office.

When Howard and his entourage arrived in our conference room, he seemed tired and uninterested. When Maureen offered him a cup of coffee, he politely declined with a slight snub of his nose. When she mentioned it was Starbucks, his eyes lit up. We served his favorite brew in a traditional glass plunger and he sipped a cup through the entire presentation.

During that trip, Howard interviewed a half-dozen PR firms to promote the opening of his Beverly Hills store. I bet their ideas were as good as ours. But in the end, Howard hired us because of a little thing.

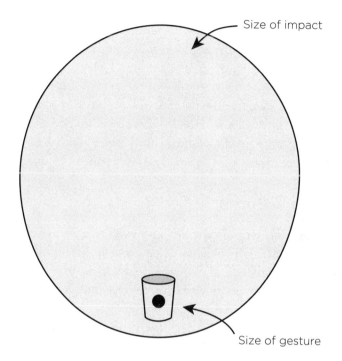

Be humble

The same year we introduced Starbucks, we launched a line of disabled dolls for Mattel, called Hal's Pals. Hal was a one-legged skier and each of his cuddly friends had a different disability — one was blind, one wore a hearing aid, and one rode in a wheel chair. This was a big departure for the company that created Barbie, and an opportunity to change the perception of children with disabilities. All of the proceeds from the sales of Hal's Pals were donated to charity through the Mattel Foundation.

Because of the sensitive nature of this project, we worked closely with the chairman of the company and the head of global communications, Spencer Boise. Our work culminated in a press conference attended by every major children's charity at a famous ice cream parlor in New York City. The kick off was a huge success. Media from all over the world wrote about Mattel's revolutionary line of dolls and their potential impact on society.

A few days later, I received a letter from Spencer, an icon in the PR industry. He stated that our work had generated the most positive press Mattel had ever received for a new product. He went on to say that he was most impressed after the event, when I carried a big cardboard box full of dolls five blocks back to their room at the Plaza Hotel. I'd worked for six months on the highest-profile product launch in the toy industry, and what he remembered most was definitely a little thing.

Solve problems

Anyone who has worked for tips knows that real customer service is about solving problems. If you're a waitress, it might be customer's food allergy. If you work at McDonald's, it might be pickles on a quarter pounder. If you're a bartender, it might be a bad bottle of wine. As a doorman, my favorite problem was people who didn't want to valet park their expensive cars. I saved a few parking spots right in front of the hotel just for them. Solving that problem several times a night doubled my income.

Men and women who solve the most critical problems are the most highly valued and compensated. I have worked at every level in my company. When I first started out, my primary responsibility was executing a task that someone else assigned me. Whether it was writing a report, organizing an event or researching a budget, my bosses evaluated me on accuracy and efficiency. I was more likely to create a problem than solve one.

In my job now, I rarely do tangible work. I mainly solve problems—with disgruntled employees, poorly performing offices, challenging prospects, demanding bosses, frustrated vendors, and unhappy clients. Sometimes I find myself wishing there weren't so many problems, until I realize if that were the case, no one would need me. Problems are the key to a long, rewarding career because there are always so many of them.

Be a problem solver!

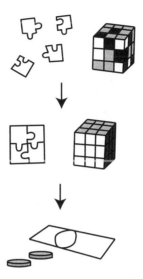

Don't wait for problems to find you. Hunt for them. Pretend they're Sudoku puzzles and see how many you can solve in a day, a week, a year. Then market your problem-solving skills on the job and in interviews. No matter what position you're applying for, when someone asks what you are best at, reply, "I'm a problem solver." If you've worked for tips, you'll have plenty of examples.

Disarm assholes

The world is full of unpleasant people, who escalate problem solving to Soviet-style diplomacy—which means you get to test your negotiating skills. Think of your interactions with jerks as master classes in the art of client service.

I learned a few such lessons in front of the Biltmore. One busy Saturday night, Mayor Tom Bradley attended an event in the Crystal Ballroom and his plainclothes LAPD escorts decided to park their unmarked police cars in front of the hotel, usurping the high-priced real estate we saved for our best customers. When I politely explained my dilemma, they refused to move, even though they could've parked anywhere. Therefore, I had no choice but to load and unload all of the other cars on the street around them. As a result, a few hours later when the mayor was ready to leave, the police cars were completely hemmed in.

Although I found the situation rather humorous, the officers were not amused, which must be why they arrested me. I was standing in front of a four-star hotel, wearing my top hat and tails, with my arms handcuffed behind my back and the LAPD screaming in my face. Then things really got bad. Because I was unable to radio drivers to pick up the cars, all the arriving guests were forced to park in the middle of the street, further surrounding the mayor. Once the three-lane street was completely blocked, the officers realized they could either book a suite for Mayor Bradley or release me. Slowly, I regained control of the situation and my new friends sped away.

Hopefully, the assholes you encounter won't be armed and dangerous, but they may be just as unreasonable. Here are a few tips for disarming them. First, don't argue. No matter how right you are, trying to convince them they're wrong just makes them angrier. Second, don't take anything they say personally. You have to realize they behave this way all the time. If it weren't you, they would be screaming at someone else. Be grateful for the practice. Third, listen. Most of the time, they aren't looking for a solution. They just need to vent. If you let them, they will eventually calm down. Then you can apologize.

"I'm sorry" is the most powerful phrase in the English language and probably French, German, and Chinese, too. Repeated ten times, it can stop a dictator dead in his tracks. You're not admitting you're wrong. You're simply saying that you're sorry something bad happened and you understand why they're angry. People and companies make mistakes. When they do, they should apologize. In my own career, I'm sorry I didn't do it more of often.

Once you've calmed them down by listening and apologizing, make one more important gesture. Give them something. Assholes love free stuff, and will often throw a tantrum just to see what they can get. You can usually disarm them with a free

How to disarm an asshole, in two words:

"I'm sorry!"

bottle of wine, a discount on their bill, extra frequent flyer miles, or a complimentary colonoscopy. In fact, this will make them so happy they'll come back again and again.

Don't be a pimp

Sometimes customer service can go too far. One quiet evening, an unassuming hotel patron asked my friend and fellow doorman where he might find a female companion for the evening. Aiming to please, Mike pulled a card from his wallet and phoned the woman who had given it to him a couple of weeks earlier. Once she entered the hotel room, the undercover policeman arrested her for prostitution and Mike for pandering. I bailed him out of jail the next morning and Mr. Duncan fired him that afternoon.

Like many people who work in service industries, Mike thought his job was to deliver whatever would make his customer happy. In his mind, calling a girl was no different than calling a cab. He was wrong. Every profession has lines that shouldn't be crossed. Even though they may be invisible, you need to figure out where they are.

Early in my PR career, I was working on a press release announcing that one of my largest clients was planning to participate in a major industry trade show. Due to deep-rooted competitive issues, the senior vice president of marketing demanded his company be referred to as "*the* industry leader," which was technically not accurate. Afraid of offending its other members, the industry association insisted that they be referred to as "*an* industry leader." Caught in the middle of a heated dispute over a single word, I informed my client that the association refused to approve his version of the release. He replied, "Send it out anyway." When I explained I didn't feel comfortable doing that, he yelled into the phone, "Who the #$@% is paying your bills?"

As you may suspect, I sent out the version he wanted, which prompted an angry call from the association president. My client apologized profusely, blaming the entire incident on me. On my ethical radar, this was barely a blip. In fact, we even laughed about it years later. But it did leave a bad taste in my mouth, because I knew I'd crossed a line.

Be careful not to cross the line

You should work hard to keep your customers and your bosses happy, but beware of going too far in the process. In the age of transparency, when CEOs are fired for falsifying restaurant receipts, there is no future in being a pimp.

There is also no future in working for a pimp. The more I got to know Mr. Duncan, the less I respected his phony, obsequious character. Our mutual dislike reached a breaking point when he terminated me for allegedly skipping my assigned shift. Not willing to take such an accusation sitting down (doormen aren't allowed to do that), I complained to the Service Employees International Union, which I discovered was part of the powerful Teamsters organization.

My first and only union experience was very satisfying. They sent a hard-as-nails, big-as-a-house female arbitrator to the hotel to investigate my grievance and arbitrate the decision with Mr. Duncan, the head of human resources, and the hotel general manager. Using copies of our work calendar as her only exhibit, she was able to prove that the doormen, not Mr. Duncan, historically developed their own weekly schedules. According to *our* schedule, I wasn't supposed to be at work the day he thought I was playing hooky.

Thanks to collective bargaining and an inept boss, the union forced the hotel's management to give me my job back and compensate me for the time I'd missed. This meant Mr. Duncan, who now hated me more than ever, had to wait six more months before he could fire me again. The second time I didn't protest because Caroline's singing career was finally paying off and I didn't need any more tips.

A few years later, I ran into Mr. Duncan when I was representing the Beverly Hills Hotel, where he was the concierge—a major upgrade from downtown Los Angeles. On the way to a business meeting with the hotel manager, I reintroduced myself to my old boss in the lobby and shook his limp hand. At first he didn't recognize me in my snappy blue suit. But when I told him I was now representing his hotel, the only words he could muster were, "What a nightmare!"

With the exception of Mr. Duncan, during my two years at the Biltmore I earned a living by making people feel welcome and important. The techniques I employed with casual tourists and harried businessmen are still applicable to my career.

Not long ago, my wife Cheryl and I were visiting Al and June Golin's apartment at the Ritz Carlton in downtown Chicago. The following day, their concierge Theresa mentioned to Al that she recognized me from my days as a doorman at the Biltmore, where she had worked as Mr. Duncan's assistant. Al scoffed at the idea saying, "That's impossible. That man is the CEO of my company!" He didn't realize that being a doorman is how I got to be CEO.

If you've worked for tips, you have an advantage over the average executive. You understand what people want. You recognize the little things that make them happy. And you know how to solve their problems. You just have to figure out how to make those tips work for you.

7.
Drive a Drunk

In 2012, Mark Zuckerberg took Facebook public, in an IPO that valued the company at $100 billion. Because of the movie *The Social Network*, we all know the story of how he created his enterprise in a dorm room. He conceived (or stole, depending upon who you believe) the idea that his Harvard classmates would like to connect with each other online. He was right. Today, 99 percent of US college students use Facebook to communicate with their friends, and Mark is a folk hero.

What does Facebook have in common with Dell, Reddit, Google, Yahoo!, WordPress, Microsoft, Napster, and even FedEx? They were all founded by students. We all dream up ideas for new products and services. We discuss them over beers. We sketch them out in notebooks. We think of clever names. We even reserve their URLs. But we rarely make them happen. Not because we don't have the money, the time, or the talent. Mark proved we can borrow those. The real reason is fear. We're afraid to fail.

We should all have at least one significant screw-up in our careers. Remember Steve Jobs's NeXT? Bill Gates's Zune? Rupert Murdoch's MySpace? Neither does anyone else, and all of these guys managed to survive. I know from experience that failure will expand your mind and strengthen your heart, even if you lose your ass.

Like Zuckerberg, I was inspired by a girlfriend—one who had been arrested for drunk driving in Los Angeles. After spending $15,000 fighting the charge, she lost both the case and her driver's license. The tolerance for this type of behavior was at an all-time low and the penalties were at an all-time high. Drunk driving was a massive problem that needed a creative answer and I believed I had one.

I called it "Sober Chauffeur, a Discreet Service for the Drinking Class." The concept was simple. After a few drinks, customers called our number and we sent a uniformed chauffeur to drive them home in the comfort of their own car. Our happy patrons eliminated the risk of being arrested and avoided the inconvenience of leaving their vehicles behind. I figured this elegant solution would be especially appealing to Angelenos, who worship wine and often drive their expensive cars 20 miles to reach their favorite restaurants.

I launched this venture from the dorm-room-sized basement of my little house in seedy Echo Park, with an attractive brochure that was designed by my friend Eric Monson and featured my doorman buddy Mike Connors in dapper chauffeur attire. I distributed the brochure along with a press release describing my new service to all the local media. The reaction was immediate. Everyone loved the idea!

Ten local news crews filmed me in my makeshift office, radio stations across America called to interview me, several national talk shows invited me as a guest, the *Wall Street Journal* ran a front page story, and syndicated columnist Bob Greene declared in the *Chicago Tribune* that Sober Chauffeur was "the best idea to ever come out of crazy California."

While the publicity for Sober Chauffeur was going gangbusters, the promotion of the company hit an early snag. Hunting for affluent customers in their natural habitat, I took a stack of brochures to the fancy bars of Beverly Hills, where the drinking upper class resides. I targeted trusted bartenders who were most likely to recommend my new service to their loyal patrons. Over a glass of Cabernet, I explained how the service operated and gave them information to distribute to their inebriated customers. As I went from bar to bar, the response got more enthusiastic, and I got more inebriated—until I noticed flashing lights in my rear view mirror. After making me walk a semi-straight line and touch my nose with my eyes closed, the Beverly Hills police arrested me for drunk driving. Through the little window inside my padded cell, I watched the cops laugh hysterically as they passed around my Sober Chauffeur business card. I've never been more humiliated, or more hungover.

Sober Chauffeur was off to an inauspicious start, but I didn't give up, even when the court suspended my driver's license for one year. Because I was one of the primary drivers in my fledgling company, I was forced to improvise. Using a Xeroxed copy of a birth certificate that my former Bar-B-Q Records partner had inadvertently left behind on a visit to LA. I recreated myself as Mark Bingham, complete with Social Security card and California driver's license. By day I was Fred, small business owner and media spokesperson. By night I was Mark, courteous chauffeur for people who couldn't remember my name anyway.

In Hollywood, where everyone has a stage name, I thought my scheme was an acceptable solution to a business problem. But I was wrong. Trying to save my company by doing something illegal could've landed me in jail for a lot longer than one night. Desperation has motivated many prominent executives to take desperate measures. Don't be one of them. Breaking the rules is different than breaking the law.

Launching my first start-up, I learned important lessons and overcame challenging obstacles. But in the end, the mentality of my clientele defeated me. As it turns out, drunks are not reliable customers. They would call in the early evening to make sure we were available later that night, but after a few drinks they never called back. We did service a handful of regulars who had been arrested four or five times and knew the next time meant divorce or prison. But even these sorry souls would get too drunk to call and invariably get popped again. After the initial burst of celebrity, the business bumped along for almost two years, until I got tired of sitting around every night waiting for the phone to ring and disconnected it.

Did I fail? Probably. Did I gain valuable experience? Definitely. Did my failure contribute to my eventual success? Absolutely. Everyone agreed that Sober Chauffeur was a groundbreaking idea that might have solved a serious societal problem. Maybe it was just ahead of its time. Today, it could've been Uber.

Although I didn't make much money, I did gain expertise as CEO, director of marketing, head of human resources, media spokesperson, and part-time chauffeur. My portfolio of press clippings impressed prospective employers. My on-camera appearances honed my spokesperson skills. My direct marketing outreach to bartenders taught me not to drink and drive.

Today, most people get their first taste of business through internships, which are mandatory for goal-oriented college students, many of whom intern every summer. I'm the first to agree that internships are useful learning experiences that often lead to full-time employment. We hire about half of our interns. But getting a good internship can be as hard as getting a good job. And in a weak economy, you can work at a half-dozen internships and never convert one into a permanent position. If you do, it will always be entry level. Being an entry-level employee at someone else's company will teach you a lot about business, but imagine how much you might learn from being president of your own.

Most corporations are cautious about taking on new employees. They've cut back on their recruiting efforts and are only hiring exceptional candidates who will have an immediate impact on their growth. Ambitious people who are willing to risk everything to build a business. In short, entrepreneurs. Whether they're self employed or employed by a big company, they don't

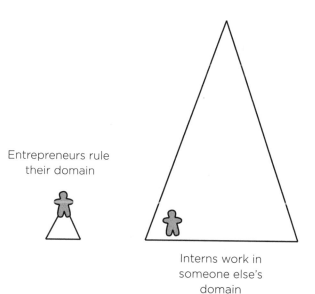

Entrepreneurs rule
their domain

Interns work in
someone else's
domain

just show up for work. They *live* for work. Which is why they always have jobs.

If you become an entrepreneur, one of three things will happen. You'll dream up a brilliant idea and execute it perfectly, venture capitalists will write big checks to fund it, you'll take your company public, and buy your own island. Or you might create a more modest enterprise delivering just enough profit to pay your rent, and if you invest more time and energy, maybe you'll be able to quit your day job. Or like me, you'll have an original concept that turns out to be a total bust. You'll lose a little money and gain a lot of experience, which you'll leverage to get a stable job at an established company.

Develop your idea

Jeff Bezos was 30 years old when he had the idea to sell books online. Today, that concept seems pretty basic, but in 1994, it was revolutionary. Like many others, I lost my ecommerce virginity on Amazon. I remember timidly typing a credit card number into my computer and my excitement a few days later when a book magically arrived at my door. I even bragged about it to my friends.

Once Jeff realized people would buy books over the internet, he opened a music store. A year or so later, when he decided to open a video store, he hired GolinHarris. We helped him expand into movies, tools, toys, groceries, clothes, and eventually anything you wanted to buy. Not every idea was a hit. He tried auctions to compete with eBay, but he was too late. When Jeff ran out of products to sell, he sold Amazon's excess computing power and became the leader in cloud computing. In his spare time, he buys newspapers, launches rockets into outer space, and dreams of drones delivering packages.

Jeff is filled with ideas, and through trial and error he figures out how to execute them. He never worries about failing. In the beginning, when people questioned him about Amazon's volatile stock price, he recommended they not buy it. Unfortunately, I took his advice.

Everyone has an idea

Don't be afraid to run with yours!

Don't be afraid to translate your concepts into reality. Every year entrepreneurs launch more than a half-million small businesses in the United States. Lots of them are started by students who, when they aren't studying, spend their time creating apps, printing T-shirts, customizing bicycles, repairing mobile phones, designing software, and making jewelry. Most of them don't make a profit, but they're all entrepreneurs.

If you already have a job, you can write your business plan in the evening, lay the groundwork on the weekend, and find a partner with the time to run it. Even if you don't strike it rich, you will gain valuable acumen that will definitely boost your career. Every company needs people with innovative ideas, ahead-of-the-curve skills, and a little courage.

Produce a prospectus

Starting a business isn't a huge commitment. I've started a couple with nothing more than a business card. But you should have a plan.

Begin by translating your idea into a single sentence and see if it makes sense when you read it. Then try it out on your friends. If your idea passes their smell test, develop a four-page proposal that explains your rationale, analyses your target audience, outlines the resources you'll need, describes how you'll market your products or services, and projects how much revenue you'll generate. Ask a professor or an entrepreneur to critique your plan. Format it to look impressive. So far you'll have invested less time than it takes to complete every level of *The Legend of Zelda*.

Jeff Bezos developed his plan for Amazon while driving cross-country to Seattle. Fred Smith's graduate thesis was the foundation for FedEx. Jessica Streitmater, a student at the University of New Hampshire, entered her business plan in a competition. She used the $5,000 prize money she won to start a web service, called Regaalo, that allows parents to send care packages to their kids in college. Based on initial sales, she and her partner have raised more than $200,000 from private investors.

If you can create an effective business plan, you'll be way ahead of most executives. You can add it to your resume or send it to angel investors.

Find funding

Once you have a good idea and a viable plan, you'll need funds to get started. Service businesses like Sober Chauffeur don't require much capital because you're selling your time or someone else's. I had a dozen employees who worked on commission. I only paid them if I made money. My only real expenses were marketing materials and a few chauffeur caps. What can you do with your spare time that other people will pay for? Train, teach, design, bake, build, or even drive. There are lots of options.

Celeste Currie knitted her way into business. She started a company called SoulScarf, combining fashion and charity. For every handmade wool scarf sold, she gives 20 percent of the proceeds to a charity of the customer's choice. She donated more than $2,000 in the first three months.

If you invent a new product, you'll need funds to manufacture it. You can borrow the cash from your parents or ask your friends to invest. You can also raise money from strangers on crowdfunding websites like Kickstarter, which connect you with individual investors who finance start-ups in exchange for products or future rewards. You can even audition for *Shark Tank* and try to convince celebrity investors like Mark Cuban to underwrite your enterprise. If you have a good idea and solid business plan, chances are someone will fund it.

Your business might need funding to take off

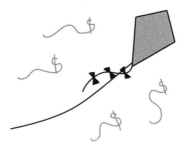

When he graduated second to last in his high school class, Jimmy John Liautaud's father gave him the choice of joining the military or starting a business. Liautaud chose the latter and accepted his father's $25,000 loan to start a hot dog business. Today, he is responsible for 1,600 Jimmy John's gourmet sandwich shops in 41 states.

Most of the companies that hit the jackpot these days are online. Groupon, Instagram, Zynga, Snapchat, and Reddit are good examples. Online businesses are easier to start because they don't require a product, a building, or a lot of employees. You just need a talented developer who can translate your concept to the digital domain.

Even if you fail, there's an intrinsic value in creating an online enterprise. Every corporation knows their future is online, but many don't know how to get there. They're desperately looking for savvy designers, programmers, and developers who will point the way.

One of GolinHarris's most talented social media experts, Len Kendall, left our firm to start a venture called CentUp, which is essentially a "like" button that can be added to any site. If a visitor likes the content being offered on a blog, or the cause being promoted on a website, she can donate a penny by simply clicking on the logo.

Len was able to get a college buddy to fund his venture in exchange for spending 50 percent of his time building a social media presence for his friend's trucking company. He dedicates the other half of his time to developing cutting-edge fundraising software that he believes will benefit mankind. Len may be the next Jeff Bezos. But if he isn't, I would love for him to return to our agency with all of the knowledge he's gained as an entrepreneur.

Market yourself

It is no surprise that a lifelong PR guy would think promotion is critical to building a successful business. Whether I was marketing records or chauffeuring drunks, getting attention from the media was the only way I could afford to tell my story. Nothing strengthens your personal brand more than positive media coverage. It's remarkable that more schools aren't teaching it and more executives aren't doing it. There are a few notable exceptions.

Promotion can help your career soar

Steve Jobs was the most media-savvy CEO I've ever met. I had the "pressure" of working with him in the *Toy Story* days of Pixar. Before Disney paid $9 billion for the company, they controlled distribution and marketing for all Pixar films. Steve didn't like being controlled. He worried that Michael Eisner was getting too much credit for the unprecedented success of the movies John Lasseter was producing. Planning for the day when Pixar would be an independent movie studio, he hired our agency to build greater recognition for their lesser-known brand.

Because he believed in the power of publicity, Steve attended every PR meeting, all of which were memorable. I recall a particularly tough session when he berated his communications team for an article about Pixar's earnings in the *New York Times*. In his view, it was an unequivocal failure, not because it wasn't accurate, but because it wasn't on the front page.

At the close of the meeting, Steve offered to take my colleague and me on a tour of the new Pixar campus, which was still under construction. Jumping at this unexpected invitation, we followed his big black Mercedes to Emeryville, California, a few miles from the drab industrial park where Pixar was founded. For the next hour, the terrible tyrant turned into an excited schoolboy as he shared every detail of his masterpiece, from the metal walkway connecting the offices to the handcrafted pizza oven he personally designed for the employee cafe. Although Steve wasn't the creative force behind Woody and Buzz, he was clearly the inspiration for their new home.

Jobs had the same unbridled passion for media. One of the most mundane aspects of the communications business is the development of a media list, which is simply the names of the reporters and publications that we are going to approach with a news story. Most senior executives leave that type of work to their minions. Not Steve. He analyzed every name on the chart and every story angle that we were planning to pitch to them. As he thumbed through the list, he would stop at certain media outlets and say, "I'll take this one." Meaning he would personally make the call to that reporter.

Never before or since have I encountered a CEO who was willing to make the effort to develop close personal relationships with the journalists who covered their company. Steve simply picked up the phone and called them. When you think about it, the idea makes perfect sense. Who did Walt Mossberg at the *Wall Street Journal* want to hear from, an account executive at GolinHarris or Steve Jobs?

Steve had a short list of outlets he felt were truly important. Interestingly, the guy who paved the way for social media was mainly interested in print. In fact, his favorite publication was *Time* magazine. Whenever he had big news, his first call was to *Time*. Not only did he pitch the story, he also demanded that he be featured on the cover, which he was eight different times — including the week after he died.

When I was getting started, I used to carry my press clippings to every job interview. Today, I have my own blog, Facebook page, Twitter feed, and Pinterest board. Imagine all the places you can tell your story, if you aren't afraid to pick up a phone or a mouse. Whether at the top or the bottom of the career ladder, we can all learn from Steve Jobs. He understood the power of the media and how to use it to his benefit. If you follow Steve's approach, maybe someday *Time* will put *you* on their cover.

8.
Guide a Tour

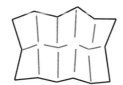

Every night at clubs like the Improv in Los Angeles and Second City in Chicago, aspiring comedians make improvising look easy. Drawing from their own experiences, these professionals use cues from the audience and their fellow performers to craft a coherent narrative that leads to a logical conclusion and entertains along the way. Improvising requires skill and practice. I should know. I've been doing it all my life.

Many job hunters worry they lack the necessary credentials. Those hoping to change careers are concerned their experience isn't relevant. These are legitimate fears, but they can be overcome. When you reach the top, everything you say and do will be scrutinized by the press and the public. Luckily, on the way up nobody pays much attention, which allows those of us who lack the standard business prerequisites to exercise a little creativity.

Lack of experience never inhibited my pursuit of a new career. After spending too many nights driving drunks, I thought it would be refreshing to spend a few weeks guiding tours. There was one small challenge: I had never been on a tour, much less guided one. Since I had no legitimate credentials, I created a resume that carefully reshaped my exploits as a cabin boy, doorman, and chauffeur to fit the mold of the travel industry.

As a chauffeur, I occasionally toured visitors around LA in their own cars, describing the sites along the way. Workable. As a doorman, I dealt with affluent tourists from all over the world and often recommended restaurants and attractions. Usable. Although it wasn't actually a cruise, I did attend to the needs of a boatload of Norwegians on their way to Asia. A stretch. Putting it all together, I had the beginnings of a decent resume. Then I crafted a series of customized cover letters, explaining why I would be a world-class tour guide.

Once I transferred my tourism experience to paper, I headed to the Los Angeles County Library to look up the names and addresses of the biggest tour operators in America. A few stamps later, I was in business. The following month, an executive from industry-leader Olson Tours called to ask if I was available to guide a busload of tourists on their "California Adventure" tour—a ten-day excursion through the state where I happened to live. A week later—without going through either an interview or a security check—I checked into the Disneyland Hotel, where I met 45 elderly people who had paid several thousand dollars each for me to escort, educate, and entertain them on their summer vacations. The first thing I learned is that improvising requires homework.

I packed my suitcase with a dozen guidebooks about stops on our trip—like Big Sur, Yosemite, and Hearst Castle—that I'd never visited. Once I had tucked my charges in safely for the night, I prepared for the next day's activities by copying pertinent facts onto index cards. Since I survived college by cramming the night before every exam, I was comfortable with the process, even though it distracted me from the Holiday Inn nightlife.

The next morning, standing at the front of the bus with my official tour guide microphone in hand, I convincingly recounted the population of San Francisco, the height of Half Dome, and the timing of the Gold Rush. When a more complex dissertation was required, I would slump down in my front-row seat out of view of my fellow passengers and recite a highlighted passage from one of my guidebooks.

The first stop on our tour was for lunch at a roadside restaurant and casino just across the Nevada border. After a 90-minute eating and gambling break, the casino owner stuffed a wad of cash into my hand. At first I was surprised, until I realized I was now the beneficiary of the global economics I'd witnessed at Enzo's Pelleteria Palazzo Vecchio.

We've all been advised that if you don't know something, just say so. That may work for driving directions, but not in the business world, and certainly not on a tour. Tourists ask a million questions and they expect their guides to know the answers. Every time I replied, "I don't know," my credibility declined—along with my tips. When I had no idea what the right answer was, I improvised.

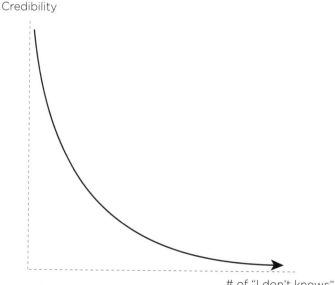

Credibility

of "I don't knows"

For the meaningful questions, like "What is the ethnic makeup of California?" I consulted my note cards. For the trivial ones, I followed the lead of my bus driver, who had 20 years of improvisation experience.

Because we spent many hours motoring across the countryside in our luxury coach, we drove by lots of foliage. Inevitably, one of our bored passengers would ask the name of a particular passing plant. Our driver, who didn't have a botanical bone in his body, always recited the same answer, "It's a bytheroadodendron." I knew he'd repeated this line a thousand times, but it still elicited a nod of appreciation.

I was asked another classic question during a visit to an historic battleground, which can be a factually challenging encounter for a novice tour guide. Once-famous scenes of heroic drama, which are now mostly empty fields, require a lot of colorful narrative (and homework) to bring them to life. As we were finishing our walking tour, one of my inquisitive flock pointed to a bunch of boulders stacked under a nearby tree and asked, "Are those the original rocks?"

"Original" is part of the tourist lexicon, meaning "was this painting, chair, or house here when some famous event happened?" In essence, he was asking whether this particular pile of rocks was sitting under that particular tree during a battle that took place 150 years ago. Without conducting carbon dating on every stone in the vicinity, no one could really know the answer to his pointless question, but I gave him one anyway.

"Yes," I said. Then he smiled and got back on the bus.

When you are starting out in business or as a tour guide, people are going to ask you a lot of questions. Some will be smart and some will be stupid. My advice is to respond to them all, whether or not you know the answer. I'm not suggesting you lie. I'm suggesting you improvise. I didn't lie about the original rocks. I used the information available at that moment to make the most logical assumption. In the end, my customer was happy and I looked smart, which is always the desired outcome.

As a tour guide, I learned how to navigate with minimal information. A few days into the trip, I discovered the entrepreneurial aspect of my job. I was allowed to organize "optional" events that were not listed in the brochure and charge extra for them. After we arrived at the Flamingo Hotel in Las Vegas, my tourists had a free evening to do something on their own. Since most people who take group tours don't want to do anything on their own, everyone signed up for my "Vegas by Night" excursion through the history and highlights of Sin City, conducted by someone who'd never been to Las Vegas.

As soon as everyone was checked in, I jumped into a taxi parked in front of the hotel. Luckily, Las Vegas cab drivers know how to find anything. For the next two hours, mine guided me up and down the strip explaining the lure and lore of his hometown—from the fall of Bugsy Siegel to the rise of Steve Wynn, all of which I scribbled furiously on my note cards. We stopped at all of his favorite casinos—Circus Circus, Golden Nugget, Caesar's Palace—long enough for me to run in, get the lay of the land, and gather a few essential facts. We arrived back at the hotel just as my group was filing back onto the bus. I discreetly handed my helpful cabbie $100 and thanked him for the information, which I repeated verbatim to my attentive troupe for the next four hours.

We ended our tour with an optional $50 dinner in Sausalito overlooking San Francisco Bay, where we all said goodbye and each couple handed me and the bus driver a final tip, usually about $20 for me and $10 for him. I assumed a more experienced tour guide made a lot more. But from my perspective, the trip was a resounding success, since no one got sick, lost, robbed, or accosted—with the possible exception of an Israeli girl who spent a few nights in my room.

As advertised, my California tour was truly an adventure, filled with instructive anecdotes that have guided me throughout the rest of my career. By the end, I realized that with a little preparation and a lot of creativity I could convince anyone of almost anything. Proving my point, two weeks later Olson asked me to lead their "American Heritage" tour through historic sites like Gettysburg, Yorktown, and Philadelphia—more places I'd never been. I checked out another set of guidebooks from the library and headed off to Washington, DC.

Thankfully, some enlightened legislator interested in tourist protection passed a law stating that local guides were mandatory at all historic landmarks. This meant that at most of the stops, someone who actually knew something about our destination would join our group, providing a steady stream of information to my busload of history buffs. However, on certain unfortunate occasions, they had to rely solely on my improvisation skills. For example, I guided them through a fascinating historical re-enactment of the famous battle of Yorktown, informed by a bro-chure that I snagged at the tourist information center while they waited patiently on the bus.

Many people think improvising means making things up, on the spot, without any advance preparation. I prefer a different definition: creating something special from whatever ordinary ingredients happen to be available. Whether you're grasping for your first job or hanging on to your last, improvisation is a man-datory skill in the business world and anyone can learn it.

Reinvent resumes

I have interviewed hundreds of prospective employees at every level of seniority. Most had only one resume, which they handed me and every other potential employer they met—usually a bor-ing sheet of paper listing work history, educational experience, and a few personal facts.

When I was looking for work, my files were full of resumes, and every one was different. None were fabricated, but each contained enough unique enhancements to make me seem like a perfect fit for the position I was applying for. I was improvising.

Do you remember the movie *Legally Blonde*? Reese Wither-spoon played a smart but ditzy sorority girl named Elle Woods who decided to enter Harvard Law School to impress her boy-friend. In one scene, she presented her resume to a partner in a law firm, who remarked with surprise that it was pink and scented. She confidently replied, "I think it gives it a little something extra."

While I don't recommend a scented, pink resume, I do suggest giving it a little something extra. Something that will make you stand out from the hundreds of other applicants who are applying for the same job. Studies have shown that employers spend an average of six seconds scanning a resume before they decide if the candidate is worthy of consideration. Erin Turner, who manages all of our agency's social media channels, headlined her resume with "Resumes are boring. But I'm not." That convinced us to hire her and we've never been bored.

Accessorize your resume
differently for different jobs

What constitutes specialness differs for each individual. It may be an unusual hobby, a place you lived, a project you conducted, a charity you started, a story you wrote, a blog you created, a band you formed, an award you won, a campaign you managed, a language you speak, a country you visited. The last lines on your resume, about personal interests, should be more than a perfunctory list. These are the details that differentiate you.

A family friend, who looks a little like Reese Witherspoon, graduated from one of the nation's highest-ranking law schools at the top of her class. She had impeccable references and a series of impressive internships, but so did many others. During every job interview, she mentioned that she grew up on a farm in rural Virginia, where she fed livestock and drove a tractor. She is now working at a prestigious law firm, where milking a cow isn't required, but a memorable interview is.

Specialness should be accompanied by specialization. Every business has become more complex, making it impossible for one person to understand every facet. Nowhere is this more evident than the medical profession. General practitioners still treat colds and flu, but for anything more serious you want a specialist. Specialists perform delicate procedures that save people's lives and solve serious problems. You should be a specialist. Drill into your passions and skills to mine an area of expertise that you can sell to prospective employers. Companies aren't interested (or prepared) to teach you everything you need to know. They want you to teach them something you already know.

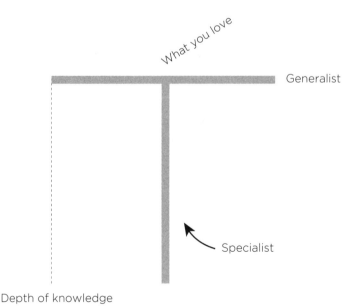

Be special(ized)!

What you love

Generalist

Specialist

Depth of knowledge

Customize cover letters

The resume format limits creativity, but a cover letter is an empty canvas for improvisation. Your words should paint a picture of who you are and convey how you will add value to their company. Don't just list what you've done. Show how your values, passions, and skills will benefit them. Remember how much time you spent on your college essay? Invest the same amount of energy writing your cover letter.

Your words should paint a picture
of who you are

This is a perfect opportunity to solicit help from your entourage. There's no law that says you have to be the sole author of your resume and cover letter. Ask the best writer you know to create a one-page masterpiece. Then revise it every time you have an interview, tailoring your message to a new audience. Actors repeat the same lines over and over. Improvisers change the dialogue in every performance.

Speaking of actors, they use video to communicate their charisma to casting directors. Why not apply this medium to getting a regular job? A professional two-minute clip brings your experience and passion to life. Elle Woods got "a Coppola" to direct her video. You should, too. Tap into your network to find a friend or colleague who has access to the right equipment and the skills to use it. When the final product is finished you can upload it to YouTube, then add a link to your resume or send it as a follow-up.

Investigate the interviewer

A recent study from Northwestern University concluded that the hiring process is a lot like dating. Hiring managers at elite professional firms tend to evaluate candidates as if they're new friends or potential romantic partners. Rather than focusing on an individual's qualifications, interviewers look for people that they would like to hang out with and whose experiences are similar to their own. Just like on a date, a spark occurs when those commonalities connect. If the interviewer ran the Chicago Marathon and discovers you did—spark. If you both lived in France—spark. If you both love to cook—spark. Three sparks and you're in.

Find interest matches with your interviewer!

Homework is the secret to igniting those sparks. The more you know about the interviewer, the more likely they'll like you. The more you know about the company, the more likely they'll hire you. The more you know about the job, the more likely it will be a good fit.

I remember interviewing one geeky graduate named Gary Brotman for his very first job out of school. He was clearly agitated about meeting me and awkward in his new suit. Gary had no previous PR experience, but he did have a three-ring binder stuffed with information about our agency and me. Over the course of our 30-minute conversation, I realized he knew more about my company than I did. Maybe he did that kind of homework for every interview. I'll never know because I hired him on the spot. Gary had an insatiable curiosity that he unleashed on every client he touched. He studied their businesses, mastered their technologies, and brought them ideas. Which is why, after five years, one of them wisely stole him away from us.

After the interview, don't send a thank-you note, especially not a handwritten one. Those are fine if you have received a gift or a bonus. But when you want a job, within 24 hours send an email that continues the conversation by addressing a point you missed or elaborating on an answer you gave. Make reference to something you were told, to prove you were listening. And remind them of the sparks.

Your follow-up email should contain...

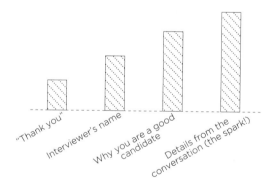

Simulate spontaneity

Media training is one of the most valuable services PR firms offer. We have coached dozens of powerful executives on how to answer tough questions from the press. By simulating ambushes and filming the results, we're teaching them to improvise. They don't memorize answers. They learn how to deliver the right message regardless of the question asked. By the end, their interviews are more like speeches, with a few annoying interruptions.

In the early days of McDonald's, when Ray Kroc had less than 100 restaurants, Al Golin would prepare him for meetings with the business press. Inevitably, the media would ask how many restaurants he planned to open. Without hesitation, Ray would deliver the answer, "One thousand." Standing in the hallway after the interview, he would wink at Al and say, "That'll be the day." Today, McDonald's has more than 34,000 locations. Ray was improvising.

Anyone can learn how to conduct better interviews by rehearsing answers to challenging but predictable (look on the internet) questions, such as: What is your greatest weakness? Why are you the best candidate for the job? What is the work experience you are most proud of? Where do you see yourself in five years? If you screw it up, don't worry. You can answer them differently next time.

Lust after openings

At certain points in your career, you may not know what you want to do next. That's okay. There is nothing wrong with figuring it out as you go along. Just don't do it during an interview. When someone asks why you think you'd be good at a job, explain why your skills are a great fit for what the company needs and why you're obsessed with working there. If you have an opportunity with Leo Burnett advertising, don't say you are contemplating a career in marketing. Confess that you're dying to work at Burnett on the Kellogg's account as a creative director, developing digital campaigns for Tony the Tiger. Then tell them why you'll be GRRREAT. If you get a better offer, you can always turn it down later. It is *your* responsibility to plan your career. The person conducting the interview is looking for hunger, not hesitation.

And don't be afraid to express some ambition. Even if you're seeking an entry-level position, proclaim that in ten years you want to be CMO, CFO, or CEO. The people currently in those jobs will be more impressed than threatened by your confidence.

Don't lie

If you graduated from Indiana University, like I did, never pretend you attended Harvard. If you got a degree in education, like I did, don't claim you majored in economics. These facts can be verified and they have caused the downfall of very powerful executives, like one short-lived CEO of Yahoo! who was fired for embellishing his educational credentials.

When you're describing your work experience, however, there is room to improvise. You are the one who can decide if you spent your time Xeroxing plans or if you were "helping to develop a national campaign," filling out nametags or "orchestrating a major fundraiser," lugging luggage or "counseling international travelers." These are your stories and you have the creative license to make them interesting.

Throw away the map

Traditional businesses thrive on predictability. Managers believe their long-term plans and linear projections will keep them on course and lead them to their desired destinations. But what happens if somewhere along the way, they lose the map?

There is no substitute for genuine knowledge—if you happen to have it. If you don't, you have to improvise. Executives make dozens of decisions every day. Proceed with a project? Invest in a business? Hire a candidate? File a lawsuit? When they have time, they conduct exhaustive research and obtain extensive advice. When they don't, they make the call based on the information in their head and the feeling in their gut. If they wait too long to make a decision, they may be too late. Companies like Nokia and BlackBerry have proven that conviction and deliberation are no match for flexibility and speed. Slow kills companies fast.

Like a Griswold family vacation, a company's journey can take unexpected turns. When it does, the ability to lead people through unfamiliar territory becomes an essential leadership skill. You can learn this. MIT offers graduate courses in dynamic leadership, taught by a former actor and director, who engages professionals of all ages in real-world simulations to hone their improvisational skills. You can practice this technique by asking yourself what you would do if you were leading an organization whose actions have landed them on the front page. Pretend you are Hillary Clinton or Jamie Dimon and try to imagine how you would react if your embassy was attacked or your bank blew a few billion dollars. Or just put yourself in a similar uncomfortable situation.

Due to a last-minute cancellation at a recent seminar, I was asked to participate on a panel discussing the "Criminalization of Internet Harassment." A member of the British Parliament, who was an expert on the subject, was also on the panel. Knowing little about the issue, I listened carefully to her point of view, then quickly extracted examples from my own experiential database that I thought might be relevant or entertaining. Although no one in the audience mistook me for an expert, they didn't think I was a twit, which is always my goal. You can test your improv skills by joining a meeting with no advance knowledge of the topic being discussed and trying to make a meaningful contribution within 15 minutes. Even a couple of provocative questions can make you sound credible.

On its surface, improvisation may seem lazy and reckless, especially in my case. But improvisation, like evolution, is a critical survival tool. Based on prehistoric genetics, evolution has allowed us to adapt to long-term changes in the biological world. Relying on present knowledge, improvisation enables us to adjust to real-time changes in the modern world. Life is too fast and too complicated for strict ideologies to determine our fate. Our future leaders must learn to play it by ear. Pope Francis understands it's possible to have convictions and still be flexible. Maybe he can teach that to the US Congress.

In a world where technology, economics, and politics change as often as Facebook profiles, being president of a company or a country is a lot like being a tour guide who doesn't know exactly where he's going.

9.

Substitute

Fifty percent of college graduates are working at jobs that don't require a college degree. Seventy-five percent of Americans say they would change jobs tomorrow if they could. These are a discouraging statistics, especially if you're one of these people. But don't give up just because your current employment isn't ideal. I used my nightmare job to practice for my dream one. You can too, if you improvise.

Being a tour guide was enjoyable, but when summer ended so did my paycheck. Faced with a declining income, I was forced to fall back on my education major, and I signed up to be a substitute teacher. The LA Unified School District offered hazard pay to brave souls who were willing to venture into the city's worst schools. As one of the few male substitute teachers under the age of 50, I volunteered for assignments in inner-city high schools where no one else would venture. I was paid $100 per day to instruct gang members in South Central on the finer points of auto mechanics and home economics, where success was measured by the absence of serious injury, including my own.

Occasionally, my assignments would last for more than a day or two. Like when Wilmington Junior High took a special liking to me. Located in a working-class neighborhood in the South Bay, Wilmington was academically ranked in the seventh percentile in Los Angeles—the seventh percentile from the bottom. The students represented a cultural rainbow, including Samoan, African-American, Hispanic, and Korean kids.

I never aspired to be a teacher. I disliked the mindless bureaucracy and had little in common with the rest of the faculty, who were dedicated civil servants burned out by years of neglect. Still, I enjoyed hanging out with the students and I needed the $18,000 salary. I really wanted to work in public relations. But since I didn't have enough experience to start a career, I practiced PR at school.

In 1984, Los Angeles hosted the Olympic Games. The entire community was excited by the prospect of athletes from around the world coming to our underappreciated city. We were shocked when the Soviet Union announced its plan to boycott the event on the phony premise that LA was too dangerous. I wasn't interested in the political reasons behind this decision. However, I was looking for an interesting writing assignment for my seventh-grade English class. Consequently, we decided to write letters to the Russians, encouraging them to change their minds about Southern California and come to the Games. Since the younger kids seemed to enjoy this activity, I tried it out on the eighth graders. Then the ninth graders joined in.

After a couple of weeks, I'd accumulated a small stack of letters and an idea. I asked the principal, who seemed to appreciate my newbie exuberance, if I could borrow the empty trophy case in the main hallway. Under a paper banner announcing "Wilmington Writes Russia" in bold black letters, my students began filling the window with handwritten envelopes addressed to the Soviet Olympic Committee. In the meantime, the head of the English department got wind of my activities and asked me to explain the idea to the other teachers, who decided to join the cause.

Then I initiated my PR campaign. During my free period, I used the office phone (the only one in the school) to inform local news producers that a grassroots movement was exploding in one of the poorest neighborhoods in LA. As the trophy case filled, the media descended. Every day a different news van parked in front of the school. Reporters interviewed me and filmed my students reading their heartfelt letters. The media attention had a profound impact on my kids, who never imagined they would be on television or noticed by the rest of the world. We were having fun.

Imagination can transform a situation!

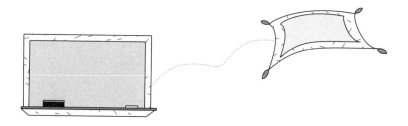

To keep the story alive, I called Peter Ueberroth's office at the LA Olympic Committee and told them we wanted them to deliver our growing mound of mail to the Russians. At first the LAOC was reluctant to get involved. When I suggested that it would look bad if they disappointed hundreds of young Olympic fans, they changed their minds. I explained that we were arranging a special delivery ceremony, and we hoped they'd send an Olympic athlete to retrieve our letters. To my surprise, they offered Rafer Johnson, a former gold-medal decathlete, to be our guest of honor. With the principal's permission, I organized an assembly for the entire student body and invited every local media outlet to cover it. A few days later, as the school band performed, my students lugged ten mail bags filled with their letters onto the auditorium stage and dumped them in a huge pile in front of Rafer and a battery of TV cameras.

I have no idea what the LAOC did with all our letters. But it was a triumphant day for the kids at Wilmington Junior High and for their substitute teacher.

After a year-and-a-half stint, I left Wilmington Junior High convinced that education is truly a noble profession. I'm still impressed by adults who dedicate their lives to teaching Shakespeare and Pythagoras to kids who would rather be playing *Grand Theft Auto*. It just wasn't for me.

But teaching taught me a valuable lesson. Instead of wasting time bemoaning a job you hate, focus on honing the skills you need for a job you want. While I was teaching kids English, I was teaching myself PR, and I leveraged that experience to start a new career.

Think outside your cube

If you look up "McJob" in the dictionary, it says "a low-paying, low-prestige job that requires few skills and offers very little chance for advancement." While there are many jobs that fit this description, some McJobs do have a future. Look at McDonald's, the company that gave them their name. Jay Leno, Jeff Bezos, and recent Republican vice presidential nominee Paul Ryan all got their start flipping Big Macs.

Many big companies find their future leaders among their current employees. More than 50 percent of McDonald's franchisees and 75 percent of their restaurant managers started out behind the counter. Today, they're all earning respectable incomes. Recently retired CEO Jim Skinner started as a restaurant management trainee in 1971 in Carpentersville, Illinois, and former president of the US region, Jan Fields, began her career as a crewmember in 1978 in Dayton, Ohio.

Jan admits there were many nights when she came home exhausted after a tough day in the restaurant and "quit in her head." But she always returned the next morning because she loved the interaction with the customers and the other employees. During three decades with McDonald's, Jan was promoted more than 20 times. Not because she asked to be. She was "too focused on doing a great job in her current position to worry about the next one." Not surprisingly, *Fortune* magazine named Jan one of the 50 most powerful women in business. No matter where you work, a McJob can turn into a McCareer if you work the system.

Figure out the best route to the top

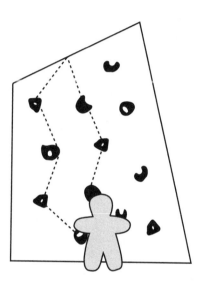

People think of their careers like ladders that they climb straight up. But sometimes the best route might require more of a sideways move, like on a climbing wall. If you aren't happy in your present position, is there another one in your company that would be a better fit? If you're impressing people in your current job, you already have a head start on the next one. You just need to convince your potential boss that you have what it takes and your current boss that she can live without you. Or you can improvise, like a cofounder of Twitter did.

After dropping out of college while on an art scholarship, Biz Stone found a first job that involved moving boxes filled with books at a large publishing firm. But Biz really wanted to work in the art department. One day while the staff designers were at lunch, he used their Mac workstations to create his own cover design for an upcoming book. He secretly slid his work into the pile of submissions on the art director's desk. When his anonymous design was selected, Biz confessed—and was promoted to full-time designer. Eventually, he left this job and went on to create the world's most powerful social network, but he got his start by thinking outside his cube.

Matt Neale and Jon Hughes thought outside their company. When their careers had run their course at our sister firm, Weber Shandwick, they volunteered to take on joint management responsibility for the much smaller GolinHarris London office. Together, they leveraged two decades of experience to create a distinct culture in a different place. Their creativity and energy won awards, as well as lots of new business, which quadrupled the size of our operation and resulted in them being promoted to presidents of our international network.

Invent a job

Wilmington Junior High had no public relations director. The teachers were more worried about paying for new textbooks than talking to the media. The school district was more interested in badgering the teachers than promoting the students. In this vacuum, I invented my own job.

Every organization has a job no one is doing, which allows you to create a position that fits your passion and expertise. If you are a fitness fanatic, conduct a company yoga class. If you are passionate about human rights, create a committee to promote diversity. If you are a sports nut, organize the office softball team. If you are a talented programmer, build a new intranet. If you are a dedicated environmentalist, create a sustainability program.

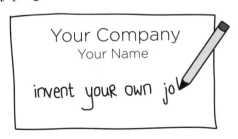

Amy George was an executive assistant at GolinHarris, but her real passion was photography. After spending her weekends taking baby photos and family portraits, she brought her camera to office events and captured images of our staff playing baseball or painting the local YMCA, which she posted on our intranet. When we developed a "Real People" marketing campaign focused on our employees, Amy volunteered to photograph the project.

Over the course of the next year, she travelled around the world, taking candid shots of different account teams engaged in work for their clients. We placed her photos in our ads, added them to our website, and hung them on the office walls. We gave Amy a substantial raise, bought her new lenses, and named her the official agency photographer—a job no one else was doing.

Compose a memo

If your ambitions extend beyond fitness and photography, write a business plan. Every company, no matter how big or small, has issues it needs to address, like product flaws, pricing puzzles, productivity declines, and marketing challenges. CEOs lose sleep over these kinds of problems and you can help solve them.

It might seem presumptuous to tackle topics the bosses can't figure out. In fact, they might not be aware of the issue, or have the time to deal with it, which gives you the opportunity to analyze the problem, investigate alternatives, interview employees, and propose a solution. You can present your results in an in-person meeting or an easy-to-read memo—like Jerry Maguire did. In either case, don't worry about getting fired, because your initiative will be recognized and rewarded.

One day while I was visiting a large wine retailer in Chicago, one of the young clerks, dressed in her purple Binny's Beverage Depot sweatshirt, nervously approached me and said her name was Hilary Jurinak. After hearing me speak at nearby DePaul University, she told me, she'd applied for an internship

If you identify a problem, write up a plan

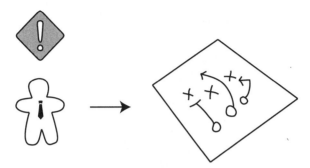

with GolinHarris, but hadn't been selected. A month after we met, Hilary sent me an email saying she'd managed to get a real job with Binny's corporate communications department.

She started by requesting an informational interview with the company's marketing director, where she shared her thinking on how Binny's could improve its online presence. He asked her to develop her ideas into a proposal, which she then presented to the president and the CEO. Impressed by her thinking, they offered her a trial position to implement her plan. After three months, they promoted her to full-time communications coordinator responsible for social media and blog content. Because she can improvise, I wouldn't be surprised if Hilary is running Binny's someday.

Donate to charity

Most organizations donate time and money to causes that are important to their customers, employees, and especially their executives. These range from massive global campaigns to cure breast cancer to smaller community programs to help the homeless. I'm proud to be part of a multi-office GolinHarris team that runs the Chicago Marathon to raise money for the Ronald McDonald House, and I cherish the friendships I build with the other runners, who otherwise I might not have known.

Find out what your company is doing to save the world and get involved. You can start by volunteering at a fundraising event.

Later, look for the opportunity to show off your philanthropic skills to senior management, who may care more about your contribution to their charity than your work for their company.

Alert the media

When I completed my Olympic campaign, I moved on to the Wilmington Drill Team. They'd won the city championship five years in a row, but few Angelenos had any idea how good they were until they appeared on the local news. When the ninth graders painted a multicultural mural on the school wall, I placed their color photo on the front page of the local paper. Think about how you can get attention for your organization and yourself.

Bloomberg Businessweek profiled a 31-year-old tech entrepreneur named Jia Jiang, who quit his job at Dell to become the "next Bill Gates" by launching a to-do list app. He was heartbroken when his only potential investor backed out. His first rejection became the inspiration for another project he called "100 Days of Rejection Therapy."

Every day he asked a complete stranger for something different. He asked a security guard if he would lend him $100. A university professor if he could teach his class. A grocery store if he could tour the warehouse. Jiang recorded his rejections and posted them on his YouTube channel, where millions of people have watched him try to take a nap in a mattress store or slide down the pole at a fire station.

Although his real job didn't pay off, his documented rejections have resulted in several speaking engagements at TED and a feature story in a national publication. Jiang is using his expertise in self-promotion to build a business helping other people overcome rejection. If your job is stalled, find a way to jumpstart it, then tell the rest of the world. Or let someone else do it for you.

A recent study by Northwestern University concluded that people who are better at bragging about their accomplishments are more likely to be viewed as leaders. While that may be true in a psych lab, I have never been big on bragging in the office. As Al Golin likes to say, "If you've got it, you don't have to flaunt it." Your entourage can do that for you, especially if you help.

One way to make it easy for them is by writing forwardable emails. When you're reporting on the results of a project you led, write the wrap-up report as if you're sending it to the president of the company. Then encourage your immediate supervisor to do just that. You deserve credit for your work, but it's better if that credit comes from someone besides you.

Execute an exit

Improvising can make your lousy job a lot better. But if you still hate it after a year, you need a plan to get out. Cubicles and classrooms are filled with frustrated people who are stuck in unfulfilling careers simply because they stayed too long. Without an exit strategy, I might still be teaching English.

My guru Daniel had a plan. After starting his career answering the phone at our LA office, he joined one of our competitors. Daniel was a talented PR guy, but his goal was to become a full-time trainer, facilitator, and executive coach. Coincidentally, a leading organizational development firm hired his agency, but after a few months was ready to walk out the door. Although he didn't service the account, Daniel offered to work for them for free in an effort to keep the client.

Over the following months, the president of the consulting company became Daniel's mentor and taught him everything he knew about organizational development. In the meantime, Daniel developed a plan to leave his agency and saved up enough money to survive on his own for six months. Today, Daniel is one of the busiest consultants in America.

Ten years ago, positions like app designer, data miner, and real-time marketing director didn't exist. The next ten years will

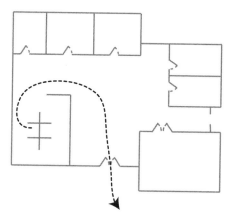

see the evolution of even more innovative jobs. Jobs that no one is doing today. If your career feels like a dead end, don't put on the brakes. With a little imagination and improvisation, you can reinvent your current job or invent a new one somewhere else.

10.
Make the Rules

Most executives rise to the top by adapting to their company's culture, by meeting quarterly financial goals, and by not getting fired. They follow a well-worn path that includes stops at an Ivy League college, Brooks Brothers, the BMW dealer, and the local country club.

How does someone from outside the corporate fraternity get accepted into this exclusive pledge class and ultimately advance to the executive suite? Sometimes you have to play by their rules. Sometimes you have to make your own.

In my twenties, I had many interesting jobs but none that could be considered a legitimate profession. When I was about to turn 36, I had no money and no prospects for making any. By that age, most of my contemporaries were far along their career paths. The fortunate ones knew before they graduated from college that they'd end up being a dentist, an architect, or an investment banker. They had well-defined goals and it was just a matter of time until they achieved them.

Some of us aren't that fortunate. We're curious about the world, but uncertain about our role in it. We're anxious to make a contribution to society, but unsure of how to do it. We're confident there is a destination waiting for us, but unclear how to find it. I discovered the most remarkable journeys unfold without a map.

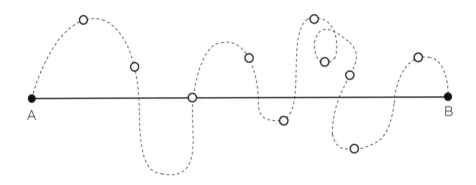

Don't be afraid to walk your own path

O Cool experiences

Clueless about life after college, my first job had been clerking in a liquor store across from the Bloomington, Indiana RCA plant where factory workers made TVs. On their break, weary men and women lined up to buy pocket-sized bottles of peach schnapps to help them through the night shift. I was happy to supply a little relief from the assembly line. Plus, I had all the free wine I could drink.

That job lasted a year. It took me 15 more to find a career.

Get class

Publicity and promotion had been integral to my work at Bar-B-Q Records, Sober Chauffeur, and Wilmington Junior High, but I didn't know anything about the public relations profession. So I went back to school.

After teaching American history to bored ninth graders all day, I rode my red Honda Hawk 20 miles across town to take night school courses at UCLA in press release writing and basic media relations. In the long run, these few classes proved more meaningful than my entire college curriculum, because my survival depended on the skills I was learning.

During my college years, I took a lot of interesting classes in college taught by colorful, passionate professors. I will always remember studying Gypsies in a folklore class, Neanderthals in anthropology, and Capulets in a class on Shakespeare. But I don't remember anyone teaching me how to get and keep a decent job. I wish Indiana University had offered courses like "Interviewing with a Prima Donna" or "Working for a Micromanager."

If you're still in school or thinking about going back, look for practical classes that are taught by front-line professionals who can share their war stories. Ask them specific questions about how they landed their first job or how they managed their worst boss. These are the subjects you need to get an A in.

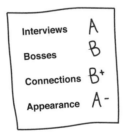

If you're trying to get a jumpstart on a new career, you can attend vocational workshops or join professional associations to immerse yourself in the field you're pursuing and introduce you to the people working in it. It's never too late to learn to be what you might have been.

Don't pay your dues

After my re-education was complete, I secured an interview for an entry-level position at a video distribution company, whose owner decided it would be more efficient to interview me and five recent public relations graduates at the same time. Sitting in a circle, we took turns explaining why we would be better than the others at writing one-page media alerts that would be distributed with two-minute videos to local TV stations. The interviewer selected her favorite candidate, then told each of us why we missed the mark. When it was my turn, she proclaimed I wasn't enthusiastic enough, which I interpreted to mean I wasn't young enough.

This demeaning experience confirmed that I wasn't cut out for an entry-level job and couldn't compete with twentysomethings salivating to do almost anything for almost no money. Recognizing it was again time to improvise, I started another business.

Thankfully, the requirements for opening my own PR agency were minimal. I only needed a phone, which I had, and a business card, which my friend Eric took care of for me. Having no real paying clients, I offered to help publicize my actress/model friend, Kathie Witt, who starred in a TV series called *Flying High*, an airborne version of *Charlie's Angels*. I also signed a small company called Tanana, started by my childhood buddy Jim Church, who thought that the next big beach trend would be scented suntan lotion packaged in plastic bananas that girls could clip onto their bikinis. I also volunteered to promote recording artists, like my hero Leonard Cohen, who were distributed by Jem Records, a small record label where my girlfriend Robyn Weiss was marketing director. Armed with this stellar client list and my snappy business card, I began my job search in earnest.

Fortunately, I had a boarder in my Echo Park house who knew a lot more about getting a legitimate job than I did. Bob Perkins had moved to LA from Washington, DC, where he was the chief fundraiser for the National Republican Senatorial Committee, which raked in millions of dollars through direct mail to help re-elect Republican senators. Despite his political affiliation, Bob was a cool guy who had been recruited to help Chiat-Day, LA's hippest ad agency, develop direct marketing campaigns for their biggest client, Apple. New to Los Angeles, he moved into my basement apartment, the former headquarters of Sober Chauffeur, while he acclimated to life in Southern California.

Bob wore expensive suits, went to lots of meetings, and worked seven days a week. Attempting to introduce me to his alien world, Bob asked one of his advertising buddies to consider me to help launch a new, long-lasting lightbulb. Although this opportunity dimmed, a few weeks later, that guy gave my name to a friend of his, who worked at a well-known PR firm called Edelman, who needed some help on the Honda motorcycle account. An avid Honda rider, I appeared the next day with a recently revised resume in hand.

Without much deliberation, an attractive 30-year-old vice president assigned me the task of creating the launch campaign for a new line of motorcycles. Having never seen an actual PR plan, I holed up in a cubicle for two weeks and typed up a bunch of wild ideas that I thought would attract the attention of the press. My first proposal must have been okay, because after presenting it to Honda, her boss offered me a job heading the agency's largest account—Kentucky Fried Chicken. Although I preferred motorcycles to chicken wings, I accepted the lofty position of account supervisor for a salary that he thought was perfect because it matched my age—$36,000. I didn't know if that amount was high or low. But I didn't bargain, because it was more than I'd ever made in my life. And I'd avoided paying my dues.

There is nothing wrong with the entry level. Candidates with graduate degrees and a fistful of internships start there. But you can make your career ladder a little shorter if you can find a way to skip the bottom rung. Starting your own business is one way to do this. Freelancing is also another option. My hourly assignment with Edelman got me in the door and ultimately into an

The career ladder is shorter if you
can skip the bottom rung

office without ever really being interviewed. If they had advertised for an account supervisor, a hundred more qualified people
would have applied. A temporary job is much easier to get than
a permanent one, and it can become permanent if you make the
right impression.

Specialization is another option. Every industry has new
frontiers. Mobile marketing, social media, big data, health information systems, international trade, cloud computing, and
green technology are a few examples. There are dozens more.
If you sharpen proprietary skills that are vital to an industry's
future, you can bypass a level or two. Generalists have a lot of
competitors. Specialists are in a field of their own.

If you're older than the competition, use your age to your advantage by showcasing tangible triumphs that can't be found in a
younger, less expensive person. Focus on your track record, not
your years of experience. If you helped your previous company
develop new products, expand into new markets, or increase
market share, demonstrate how you will do the same for your
new employer. Instead of a resume, use sales charts to tell your
story. A proven winner is a safer bet than an unproven beginner.

Dress for access

Once I was officially employed, I spent the weekend buying the first suits I'd owned since the seersucker ones with short pants my mother made me wear. I also purchased a leather briefcase and a matching pair of shoes.

What you wear may seem superficial in the age of flip-flops, but when you're making a first impression, your appearance matters. Every industry has a look that mirrors success, which you need to reflect. These days, even top college football players hire "draft stylists" to choose their wardrobe for the annual NFL event. Why shouldn't you do the same if you want to be a top pick? You can start by covering up your tattoo and getting a haircut. Because despite all the talk about nontraditional hires, most employers hire people who look just like they do.

Dress for access

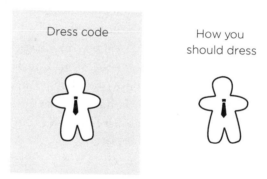

Dress code

How you should dress

I remember an enthusiastic new recruit named Chris Perez, who grew up in Inland Empire, a blue-collar region just east of the Los Angeles metro area. At the end of his first week, he asked me to help him shop for clothes that he could wear to the office. I gladly spent the next Saturday with him trying on bargain-basement outfits in the Garment District. In the end, he looked sharp in both a basic gray flannel suit and a navy blue blazer. A few years later, Chris left our agency to start his own company, which he eventually sold for a lot of money. Now he wears whatever he wants.

Think small

Learning to manage a multimillion-dollar account was easier than I anticipated. Edelman had managed the KFC business for more than a decade, and every year they just repeated the same programs—a Mothers Day card contest, a country music radio promotion, and a March of Dimes fundraising campaign. My job was to keep the franchisees happy by making sure each campaign was a little more successful than the year before.

After six months of peddling the Colonel's secret recipe, I got my first call from a headhunter—a person who is actually paid to help you get a better job. Cris Credaire explained that he was working on behalf of a small independent agency looking for someone to manage its most important clients. Since he had gotten my name from another one of Bob's friends, I agreed to meet him the following week.

Having never encountered a headhunter before, the whole experience had the feeling of an illicit affair. I snuck away from the office for a secret rendezvous at a downtown hotel. Sitting inconspicuously in the lobby, I waited anxiously for my unidentified suitor to arrive, hoping none of my coworkers would wander in and spot me. But he never showed up. Deducing that headhunters might be a little flaky, I drove back to work thinking that my current job was just fine. A few days later, Cris called to apologize, saying he'd broken his leg. After a little persuasion, I returned to the same hotel a few days later to find him wearing a cast and walking on crutches.

Headhunters aren't much use at entry level, but they can be a valuable resource for more senior positions. With a little research, you can identify the individuals who specialize in your industry. Treat them like other members of your entourage by keeping them informed of your progress and asking for their help when you need it. Even if you aren't paying their bills, you should be on their list of talented candidates.

I later discovered that Cris was actually married to his client, a dynamic entrepreneur named Betsy Berkhemer, who with her business-minded partner Richard Kline ran a small agency called Berkhemer and Kline. After a couple of one-hour interviews, they were impressed enough by my "extensive" experience at Edelman to offer me a job.

The conventional wisdom is to start at small company and move to a bigger one. After just a few months, I was moving from a large established agency where I was managing a global brand to a tiny unknown firm, where one of my clients was the BathWomb—the world's most expensive bathtub, designed by Neil Diamond's brother.

If the main road is jammed, a side route may be faster

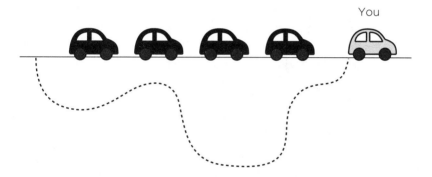

When I resigned, my boss told me I was making a big mistake, but the only other job he could offer me was the one he had. If the freeway is jammed, sometimes smaller surface streets are faster.

At GolinHarris's Chicago headquarters, Gary Rudnick was one of many aspiring young executives. When we needed someone to run our tiny Texas operation, he jumped at the chance. He spent his time in Dallas gaining management experience that would've been a long time coming if he'd stayed home. Five years later, Texas was thriving and Gary returned to apply his skills in Chicago. His title is now president of the Americas. In his case, thinking small paid off big.

Unbalance work/life

In the beginning, despite all the talk about work/life balance, I mostly worked. I greeted everyone when they arrived in the morning and was still at my desk when they left in the evening. If a client meeting ended at five o'clock, I drove back to the office to log a few more hours. I could've easily worked from home, but no one would've noticed. I also worked weekends. Because I'd gotten such a late career start, I had a lot of catching up to do.

Working long hours helped me rise through the ranks without ever asking for a promotion. I visibly reminded my bosses of my value every day, not just once a year at my review. The ratio between work and life isn't a constant. In the beginning, it needs to be more work. Later, you discover the two merge indistinguishably. Woody Allen said, "Eighty percent of success is showing up." I would add the word "early."

Unbalance work and life

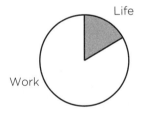

Mix carefully

I was happily married to my job when I broke another rule. I fell in love with a coworker. During the two years she worked in the Los Angeles office, I knew three things about Cheryl Cooper. She was a lot younger, she drove a Mercedes, and she dated Jerry Seinfeld. For those reasons, I never thought much about Cheryl, until one of her coworkers confided that she'd had a dream about me. This was an intriguing bit of information to learn on the day she quit to move to New York City. At her going-away party that night, I was so nervous talking to her that I dropped guacamole on her foot. On my next trip to New York, I invited her to dinner. There were many more trips. A year later, Cheryl returned to LA and to GolinHarris. Although she didn't report directly to me, we thought it was prudent to be discreet about our relationship.

Office romance is tricky. Thirty percent of workers admit to having had a relationship with a coworker, but only 5 percent of companies have policies that address the issue. GolinHarris wasn't one of them. But that didn't prevent two women in Human Resources from combing through our mobile phone bills to expose the fact that we were seeing each other. Once their detective work was complete, they cornered me in a conference room to state their findings and extract a heartfelt confession. More angry than repentant, I called my boss in Chicago, Rich Jernstedt, to explain our dilemma. Rather than being upset, he seemed genuinely happy for us. We were relieved, but we knew the situation was awkward for everyone around us. Cheryl resigned a few days later. It should've been me.

Today, CEOs and four-star generals are fired for similar indiscretions. I was fortunate to work in a more tolerant time at a more understanding company. Cheryl and I have been happily married ever since and we're still friends with our accusers. My naivete caused a lot of unnecessary anxiety, but that was the best rule I ever broke. If you're really lucky, sometimes you find yourself through a relationship with someone else.

When people spend 75 percent of their waking hours at work, the odds of developing a romantic connection with a coworker or a client are pretty high. I've seen it happen dozens of times and I've even attended a couple of employee weddings. Those couples have the advantage of innately understanding the pressures their partners face everyday.

Cheryl has worked at several rival agencies and we've often competed for the same clients. But we only ran into each other once. As my group was leaving the prospect's conference room and her team was entering, we exchanged a brief kiss in the hallway. Our colleagues were shocked, but for us it was just another day in the life. And that day, she won the account.

If you get involved with a colleague, don't keep it a secret like I did. Explain the situation to your bosses and work with them to create a structure where your relationship isn't making other people uncomfortable. When your coworkers are your friends, it's impossible to keep your personal life separate from your professional one. Just mix them carefully.

Collect coins

Careers are like video games. We all begin in the same place and advance using the tokens we accumulate. Along the way, challenging obstacles and strange enemies try to stop us. Some of our experiences move us forward to the next level. Others send us back. Every game comes with an instruction book, but intuitive players figure it out as they go along.

On the job at Berkhemer and Kline, I quickly established my independence. Company founders are hands-on entrepreneurs who like to be involved in every detail. An accomplished writer, Richard insisted on personally editing every single piece of correspondence before it left the building. The only thing missing was a letter grade. A new-business master, Betsy would spend ten minutes before every presentation playing musical chairs, until she decided exactly where everyone should sit. This level of supervision might work for someone just starting out, but I was their same age.

Richard and I were working a media reception for a small company that manufactured a nondairy creamer called Mocha Mix. When he began peppering me with questions about microphones and nametags, I simply said, "Relax, I have it under control." It must have worked, because he never interrogated me again.

To collect the most tokens possible, I jumped for clients that didn't interest anyone, including me — like the Red Cedar Shake and Shingle Bureau. This Canadian trade association was responsible for the promotion of shake roofs, which were banned in many areas of California as a fire hazard. My job was to convince homeowners and legislators that cedar shakes that had been chemically treated with fire retardant were safe. Every time a residential fire broke out, the local TV crews would race to our office to interview me as the expert on the topic. Defending wood roofs wasn't very gratifying, especially after a neighborhood full of them had burnt to the ground, but the Bureau grew to be our largest client and I owned it.

I also owned unglamorous insurance companies, accounting firms, agricultural commodities, lumber mills, and of course the BathWomb. Over time, the work gets sexier, but in the beginning, it's easier to land assignments that no one else wants. The lowliest work builds your character and your career. I collected enough tokens in my first six months at B&K to get promoted to vice president. Level completed.

A year later, Richard and Betsy announced they were selling their agency to a Chicago company I had never heard of called GolinHarris. They took a photo on the steps of a gazebo in the courtyard of our building to commemorate the partnership. The five respective founders were in the front row. I was in the last. It never occurred to them—or me—that 15 years later I would be CEO.

Ask for opportunities, not promotions

The sad truth is you think about your career every day and your bosses don't. You have a choice. You can pester them about being promoted, or you can offer to help when every new opportunity arises.

Approaching 40, I was just getting started in a profession. I'd barely graduated from an average college. I'd never taken a business course. I didn't own a golf club. I didn't know if the Giants played football or baseball. I typed with two fingers. And now, I was employed by complete strangers. Fortunately, I'd collected too many tokens for them to fire me.

Once I made myself indispensable, instead of asking for a raise, I asked to leave. This is how you advance inside your

Ask for opportunities...

And the promotions
will follow

company. First, you take on assignments, then you ask for op-portunities. These opportunities could be on another account, in another business unit, in another office, in another country, or, as a last resort, in another company. Even if you never get any of them, your offers are tokens that will help you get to the next level.

When I heard GolinHarris was looking for someone to run the struggling New York office, I immediately volunteered to move there. After a brief discussion, Betsy, Richard, and our CEO declined my offer by saying I was too valuable to the Los Angeles office, which was a nice way of saying I didn't have enough experience. I was more relieved than disappointed be-cause I didn't really want to move to Manhattan. But I'd made my point, without complaining or threatening to quit. And they responded with a promotion. Level completed.

A year later, Richard was named the firm's COO, which meant he'd be spending a lot more time in Chicago and would need someone to take on his responsibilities. This time, I offered to help him make his transition by comanaging the office with another executive. Level completed.

Two years later, Richard was promoted to run our sister firm. Tired of sharing management responsibilities, I proposed join-ing him to open the firm's California operation. Afraid to lose me, Rich Jernstedt promoted me to managing director. Seven years after joining the LA office, I was running it, without ever asking for a promotion. Level completed.

The next rung on my ladder opened up when Rich fired the company's president in Chicago. Naturally, I volunteered to move my reluctant family to the Midwest to take his job. Relocating is painful, especially if you have a family, but it was a perfect opportunity for me to reinvent myself. Level completed.

My first year in the Windy City was frustrating because no one, including me, was sure why I was there. Then everything changed. As a result of a reorganization at our parent company, we got a new boss. I'd never met Harris Diamond, but his reputation preceded him. His take-no-prisoners approach was a shock to our gentle culture and underperforming business. A few months into the job, Harris called me while I was on vacation to say I needed to return to Chicago. A few days later, in a nearby coffee shop, I became an unlikely CEO. This time, I didn't have to volunteer. I was drafted.

Was I prepared for the job? If you've read any of the previous pages, you already know.

Hustling pool exposed me to new ideas and people. Hitting the road educated me on global culture and business. Asking the captain empowered me to question senior executives. Taking a punch from a hippie guru taught me the value of listening. Failing in the music business convinced me I needed an entourage. Working for tips trained me to deliver client service. Driving drunks drove me to become an entrepreneur. Guiding a tour prepared me for improvisational leadership. Substituting schooled me on how to create my dream job. I was ready.

By condensing my career into a few paragraphs and comparing it to Super Mario Brothers, I may be giving the impression that it's easy to become a CEO. It isn't. I was very good at my job and I worked very hard at it for a very long time. But a lot of people do the same thing and never make it to the top of their companies. Sometimes the line between success and failure is inexplicable. For me, the secret was improvisation. At every level, I reinvented myself for the next role I needed to play.

Stick around

One rule you should consider breaking is jumping jobs every time you get an offer. Young professionals have been programmed to think a successful career means switching companies every couple of years. When I ask new recruits how many think they will work at our agency for more than 25 years, sadly no one raises a hand.

I left my first PR job after six months because I thought I had a better opportunity somewhere else. But I've stayed at the second one for almost 30 years. If you have a job you enjoy, in a company you respect, working with people you like, investigate the opportunities staring you in the face.

When another company is wooing you, they will inevitably promise you the moon. If your current employer hasn't fully mapped your trajectory, use your job offer as an opportunity to see what orbit they have in mind. You're not asking for anything. You're simply measuring your value. To make the most of this situation, always have this conversation before you accept a new position — making it clear that you're open to hearing what your current boss has to say. Employers are more motivated to accommodate someone who doesn't want to leave than someone with one foot out the door.

Use offers to measure your value

I once had a very lucrative job offer from a much bigger competitor. After a couple of interviews, I decided their values and culture weren't a good fit. Even though I wasn't going to move, I discussed the offer, in a nonthreatening way, with my bosses. I explained that I loved working with them but that the salary, stock options, and benefits I was being offered were tempting for someone starting a family. Even though I didn't ask, they gave me a raise, a chunk of stock, and a loan for a down payment on a house.

If you do decide to leave, you can always come back. Ellen Ryan-Mardiks has worked for GH for 30 years. In the middle of her tenure, she thought it was time to try something different and moved to a competitor. After a year, Ellen realized she'd made a mistake and returned home. Today, she is our vice chairman and manages many of our most important client relationships. Ellen is a role model for our newer people, and for sticking around. I'm always grateful that she did.

You may have to improvise to get the opportunity you want in your current job, but reinventing yourself in a company you love is better than starting over in a company you don't. Jumping from job to job is like dating—fun but not very satisfying. Growing with the same job is like marriage—not always easy but very rewarding. I could've changed jobs a dozen times and probably made a lot more money. But I would've missed the richness that only develops through a long-term relationship.

Take risks

Herb Kelleher, the founder of Southwest Airlines, is the role model for breaking the rules. He moved to Texas to open a law practice but started an airline instead. He drew his proposed triangular, three-city route on a cocktail napkin in a San Antonio bar. It now hangs framed above his desk. After four years of legal battles, Herb launched his fledgling airline in Dallas, then expanded across the country. He slashed prices, eliminated seat assignments, promoted friendly service, and wreaked havoc on the competition. Today, Southwest is the most profitable airline in US aviation history.

Herb was my favorite client because he did what he wanted and didn't give a damn what anyone else thought. He was the only CEO who dressed up like Elvis, smoked cigarettes during speeches, and, much to their surprise, kissed our female staffers on the lips. Executives from other companies and countries frequently visited Southwest's headquarters to learn the secret of its success. Whenever they asked to see the research department, Herb proudly replied that Southwest didn't have one. He believed "research was an excuse for not making a decision." Herb was improvising.

Of the dozens of wacky events we conducted with Herb, my favorite was the unconventional resolution of a trademark issue with the CEO of an airfreight company. In a dispute over the tagline "Just Plane Smart," Herb decided that an arm wrestling contest was a better option than going to court. This would be no ordinary competition. In true Southwest style, his entourage rented a Dallas sports arena complete with a regulation ring. To build anticipation for the event, we distributed a videotape of Herb "training" for the bout by curling half gallons of Wild Turkey on each arm with a cigarette dangling from his mouth.

On the big day, flight attendants wearing cheerleader uniforms incited screaming Southwest employees as Herb entered the ring is his silky boxing robe. Despite his rigorous training regimen, the much younger executive of the other firm instantly crushed him. Adding to the comic drama, a group of medics carried our losing CEO off the canvas on a stretcher to a waiting ambulance. When it was all over, Southwest generously donated the legal fees they avoided to charity and Herb's opponent graciously contributed his tagline.

If Herb sounds like a nut, keep in mind that *Fortune* magazine named him the best CEO in America. He broke all the rules and in the process built one of the most respected companies in the world. Even though his unconventional approach wouldn't work for most people, Herb proves that you can be different and still be successful.

After being CEO for a decade, I'm still making up my own rules. A couple of years ago, I decided it was time for our agency to better adapt to all of the massive disruptions reshaping the worlds of marketing, media, and technology. Our senior management team embarked on a project we called "Agency for the Future." Our goal was to redesign the entire company from the ground up to provide our clients with deeper insights, bigger ideas, and broader engagement across all channels of communication.

To accomplish this, we dismantled the hierarchical structure that had driven the firm for more than 50 years, which consisted of a dozen levels of account executives and vice presidents, all of whom did basically the same thing. We replaced that model with four distinct communities of skilled specialists. Strategists are analytical thinkers who distill data into nuggets of brilliance. Creators are experts at developing and packaging breakthrough creative concepts. Connectors are media junkies adept at telling stories across all channels. Catalysts are change agents responsible for integrating these skills into seamless campaigns for our clients.

We built a multimedia engagement center, called the Bridge, in every one of our offices to leverage the power of real-time marketing. We deploy the latest technology to analyze the trending topics of the day online and off. Then we devise spontaneous strategies for infusing our clients in the conversation as it happens. Our proprietary software monitors our insights and measures our engagement.

After a year of drafting job descriptions, creating training modules, testing technology, and developing timelines, we launched our new model under the banner of g4, representing our four specialty areas. Our mantra was PRevolve, which Urban Dictionary defines as "changing on purpose."

The response was overwhelming. The *New York Times* wrote a feature story on our evolution, followed by hundreds of other articles in marketing publications around the world. Competitors analyzed our every move. Universities invited us to speak to their students. Industry associations gave us awards. Pundits declared we were forever changing the way PR agencies operate.

Why was there so much interest in what we were doing? Because we were making our own rules. The world around us was changing, but every other media company was operating the same old way. There were dozens of editorials and panels on the future of the business, but it was all just talk. Until our sleepy Midwestern company tried something different.

Whether you're a business or a being, you must change to survive. As Martha Stewart (who also spent part of her career behind bars) said, "When you're through changing, you're through."

We discovered that innovation requires improvisation. There were no rules to follow. No books to read. No competitor to copy. No experts to consult. We had to improvise. We made mistakes and we made adjustments. We invested in new technology and we figured out how to use it. We created new training and we adapted it to meet our changing needs. We hired new people who fit our model and we fired people who didn't. We even changed our name. We're figuring it out as we go and we always will be.

The business world is full of rules. Some succeed by following them, others by breaking them. You have to find the right balance, based on who you are and who others expect you to be. If you break all the rules, you may frighten people. But if you make your own rules, they may not even notice.

EPILOGUE
Have No Fear

After reading my story, you may be wondering what your odds are of becoming a CEO. They're probably as good as mine. But that's not really the question. There are many paths to success and they all end up in different places. The real question is which one is right for you. And the only way to find that answer is to improvise.

Look for signs

I was fortunate to have the freedom to explore. I had no student loans. I could travel the world on five dollars a day. And my parents didn't complain when I tried a dozen different jobs before I finally found a career.

These days, it's harder to find an alternate route. But if you look closely, the signs are there. Sometimes the smallest ones make the biggest difference. Sure, the college you attend and the first job you choose will shape your future. But so will a weekend tennis tournament, a number in a bingo basket, a ship with engine trouble, and a coworker's dream. Random clues can lead to interesting detours. Keep your eyes open.

Remain calm

Most of us spend half of our waking hours working and the other half worrying about work. We stress about disappointing our parents, being liked by coworkers, screwing up a project, receiving a promotion, landing a better job, making more money, getting fired, and saving for retirement.

Worry less

Expectations & fears

I worried about all of these things. But it didn't matter. You can read every self-help book, attend every seminar, follow every piece of advice, work your ass off, and still never be a CEO. It's a waste of energy to obsess over arbitrary career goals. The perfect job for you may not have been invented yet. You may have to invent it yourself. Life is a sum total of your experiences not your promotions. Relax a little.

Be brave

Every commencement speaker extolls the value of pursuing your own destiny, but in the corporate world there is no real incentive to take risks. Because of the economy, student loans, and parental anxiety, there's never been more pressure to get with the program. But an ordinary life leads to an ordinary career.

It takes courage to improvise. In the beginning, you may feel shy, anxious, and intimidated, like I did. But every time you try something new you gain a little more confidence. Start by reading a different magazine, watching a foreign film, or eating lamb vindaloo. Next, send a thoughtful email to your boss or an outrageous resume to a company you're dying to work for. Then, launch your own social network. Experience builds courage.

Courage is built by experience

■ = Experience

And failure fortifies it. I was kicked off the tennis team, punched by a guru, fired as a doorman, ignored in the music business, arrested as a chauffeur, flunked as a teacher, and lost as a tour guide. These days, I don't like to fail, but I'm not afraid to.

When you take side roads, life gets a little bumpy. But signs along the way will guide you and challenges you overcome will give you the courage to continue. In the end, the trip is more interesting than the destination. Make it special.

###

ACKNOWLEDGMENTS

I owe my unlikely success to my family, friends and colleagues who have encouraged, taught and tolerated me as I have tried in my way to be free. Thank you...

Mom and Dad—for allowing me to experiment with life even when it worried you.

Steve Barnett, Mark Bingham, Jim Church, Mike Connors, Marcia Fraser, Bill Karges, Michael McCummings, Eric Monson, Elaina Nanapolis, John D. O'Connor, Dorothy Parker, Caroline Peyton, Lois Sarkisian, Dale Sophia, Jamie Stobie, Heinz Wandtke, Robyn Weiss, Rick Witt, and Gordon Woodward—for making my life special.

Betsy Berkhemer, Harris Diamond, Kristen Gabriel, Al Golin, Rich Jernstedt, Richard Kline, and John Weir—for offering me unbelievable career opportunities without any legitimate justification.

Bob Perkins—for helping me understand the business world and find my role in it.

Lee Cohen—for encouraging me to translate my random experiences into orderly advice and helping me organize my haphazard thoughts.

Liz Fosslien—for bringing my words to life with her unique perspective and distinctive designs.

Jennifer Keene—for treating me like an important client at Octagon, even though I'm not.

Doug Seibold—for believing in an unlikely, unknown writer.

Len Kendall—for reminding me to always speak in my own voice.

Molly McCullough, Karrie Towsley, and Erin Turner—for advancing this project in a hundred important ways.

All my friends at Golin—for making every weekday interesting, rewarding and "business fun" for almost 30 years.

My sister Carol and brother Robert—for being smart enough not to follow in my footsteps but supporting me at every step of the way.

Noah and Emily Cook—for giving me a reason to be successful.

Cheryl Cook—for supporting, guiding, and surprising me every step of the way. I value your advice more than my own.

About the author

Fred Cook is the CEO of Golin, an award-winning public relations agency with 50 offices around the globe. He has worked with some of the country's most fabled business leaders, such as Apple's Steve Jobs, Disney's Michael Eisner, and Amazon's Jeff Bezos. He has helped introduce the world to Teenage Mutant Ninja Turtles, Pokémon, and the seedless watermelon. Cook currently lives in Chicago with his wife, Cheryl, who works at a competing PR agency, and his son, Noah, who loves tennis and aviation. He spends much of his time in Los Angeles, where his daughter, Emily, works in casting for film and television. When he isn't working or writing, he likes to run and has completed marathons in both cities.

You can follow Fred **@fredcook** on Twitter or **fredhcook** on LinkedIn. You can also find him on Facebook at **Improvise** or on the web at www.unlikelyCEO.com. As part of Octagon Speakers, he also delivers presentations about life and leadership to audiences around the world.

About the illustrator

Liz Fosslien is the executive editor of News Genius. She also illustrates and works on building fun design systems that can be found at fosslien.com. She lives in Brooklyn, New York.